# JUSTICE IN WAR-TIME

HONORABLE BERTRAND RUSSELL

AUTHOR OF

JUSTICE IN WAR TIME

# JUSTICE IN WAR-TIME

BY

## BERTRAND RUSSELL

*Author of "German Social Democracy,"*
*"The Principles of Mathematics,"*
*"Scientific Method in Philosophy" &'c., &'c.*

CHICAGO      LONDON
THE OPEN COURT PUBLISHING CO.

1916

940.9294

# PREFACE

THE following essays, of which all except the last
two have appeared in various magazines, were written
at different times during the course of the war, and
are not perhaps wholly consistent in their expectations as to the future, or in their view as to the attitude of the ordinary citizen towards war. In such
matters, the development of events inevitably somewhat modifies first impressions. The view that the
bulk of the population is naturally pacific, and is only
incited to war by politicians and journalists, is widely
held among pacifists, but is vehemently rejected by
the more bellicose, who point out that men have an
instinct of pugnacity, which demands war from time
to time. I think it is true that many men have an
instinct towards war, but unless it is roused by its
appropriate stimulus it may well remain completely
latent. The instinct, and the machinations of war-
mongers, are both needed to bring about war; if either
were coped with, the other would be no longer operative for evil. In the following essays I have dealt
sometimes with the one, sometimes with the other; but
both are essential factors in the problem, and neither
can be neglected by any prudent friend of peace.

The first of these essays, which was written before
the Bryce Report appeared, deals in part with the
question of atrocities. Nothing in that report tends
to invalidate the conclusion reached in the article,
namely: "No doubt both German and Russian atrocities have occurred. But it is certain that they have

been far less numerous, and (for the most part) less unnatural, than they are almost universally believed to have been." Those who can recall what was believed in England in the early months of the war will acknowledge that the Bryce Report, bad as it is, tends to show that the atrocities which may be called "unnatural" have been much fewer than most English people had supposed. I think it should be added that some of the cases mentioned in the Bryce Report are admittedly based on evidence such as would not be accepted in a criminal prosecution. I have not seen the German Reports on supposed Russian atrocities, but they, if they are honest, presumably show exaggeration in what Germans believed about Russians. If the atrocities, however, were as bad as was believed, that can only increase our horror of war. It is war that produces atrocities, and every fresh atrocity is a fresh argument for peace.

The last essay is an attempt to show how England might have averted the war by a wiser policy during the ten years preceding its outbreak. To publish, in war-time, a criticism of the policy of one's own Government, is an act which will be thought by many to be unpatriotic. My own deliberate belief, however, is that what I have to say is more likely to benefit England than to injure it, in so far as it produces any effect at all. As some readers might misunderstand my motives, I have thought it well to state them by way of introduction.

I consider that either a serious weakening of England, France, and Italy, or a serious strengthening of Germany, would be a great misfortune for the civilisation of the world. I wish ardently to see the Germans expelled from France and Belgium, and led to feel that the war has been a misfortune for them as well as for the Allies. These things I desire as strongly as the noisiest of our patriots. But there are other things, forgotten by most men in the excitement of battle, which seem to me of even greater importance. It is important that peace should come as soon as possible, lest European civilisation should perish out of the world. It is important that, after the peace, the nations should feel that degree of mutual respect which will make co-operation possible. It is important that England, the birthplace of liberty and the home of chivalrous generosity, should adopt in the future a policy worthy of itself, embodying its best, not deviously deceptive towards the hopes of its more humane citizens. Because I prize civilisation, because I long for the restoration of the European community of nations, but above all because I love England, and because I have hopes in regard to England which I should feel Utopian in regard to Germany: because of these fears and these hopes, I wish to make the English people aware of the crimes that have been committed in its name, to recall it to the temper in which peace can be made and preserved, and to point the way to a better national pride than that of dominion.

The British public, under the influence of an excited Press, believes that any criticism of the past actions of our Foreign Office tends to interfere with our success in the war. This, I feel convinced, is an entire delusion. What has interfered with our success, is, first and foremost, the supreme organizing capacity of the Germans. The faults, on our side, which have retarded our victory, have been lack of ability in some of the higher commands, lack of co-ordination in the efforts to produce munitions, jobbery and family influence in Army appointments instead of the Napoleonic maxim of "la carrière ouverte aux talents" belief, on the part of our politicians, in expedients and clever words rather than a determined, concentrated vigorous effort of will. Germans who flatter themselves with hopes of England's decadence forget that we have exhibited exactly similar faults in all previous wars, and yet have been invariably victorious except against our kith and kin in America. There has been no failure of energy, courage and self-sacrifice on the part of the nation, but there has been failure on the part of its rulers. It is these same rulers, not the nation, whose past foreign policy I wish to call in question. And I do this in the hope that, after the war, England, together with France and America, may lead the world in a more just, a more humane, and a more pacific way of dealing with international problems.

It will be said in England that such criticisms as I have made of our Foreign Office are calculated to estrange the sympathy of Americans. I believe this to be an entire mistake. Both England and Germany, in presenting their case to the American public, have erred in claiming a complete sinlessness which is not given to mortals, and is not credible except to the eyes of self-love. Both have sinned, and any citizen of a neutral country will take this for granted before

beginning to investigate the facts. No history of
events which does not recognise this will command his
assent. But though both have sinned, the sins of
England sink into insignificance beside the German
treatment of Belgium. And if any Power is to be
supreme at sea, it must be better for international
freedom that that Power should be England, whose
army is too small to be a danger, rather than Germany,
which has by far the most powerful army in the
world. On these broad grounds, if I belonged to a
neutral country, my sympathies would be against
Germany. And as an Englishman, I believe that
there is far more hope of reform in the foreign policy
of my own country than in that of Germany. Most
of the somewhat discreditable facts related in the
following pages are very little known in England:
if they were widely known, they would inspire widespread horror and determination of amendment. The
same, I believe, is true of France. On this ground,
also, England and France may claim the sympathy
of America. But the best way of estranging the sympathy of neutrals is to make for ourselves pretensions
which are obviously contrary to the truth, and to
show that many among us have become blind to the
claims of justice. No good cause is served by the
suppression of truth; and those among us who show
fear of truth are doing a greater disservice to the
national cause than can be done by fearlessly proclaiming even the most damaging facts.*

---

*I have been greatly helped in the investigation of facts by
Miss Irene Cooper Willis, who, from a consecutive study of "The
Times" during the critical periods of the years concerned, has
been able to supply me with most of the references, all of which
she has also verified.

# CONTENTS.

# JUSTICE IN WAR-TIME

## AN APPEAL TO THE INTELLECTUALS
## OF EUROPE.*

Leibniz, writing to a French correspondent at a time
when France and Hanover were at war, speaks of
"this war, in which philosophy takes no interest."
[Philosiphische Werke, Gerhardt's edition, I., p. 420.]
We have travelled far since those days. In modern
times, philosophers, professors, and intellectuals generally undertake willingly to provide their respective
governments with those ingenious distortions and
those subtle untruths by which it is made to appear
that all good is on one side and all wickedness on the
other. Side by side, in the pages of the *Scientia,* are
to be read articles by learned men, all betraying
shamelessly their national bias, all as incapable of justice as any cheap newspaper, all as full of special
pleading and garbled history. And all accept, as a
matter of course, the inevitability of each other's bias;
disagreeing with each other's conclusions, yet they
agree perfectly with each other's spirit. All agree that
the whole of a writer's duty is to make out a case
for his own country.

---

*This article was written in April, before the Russian defeats,
the participation of Italy, the sinking of the Lusitania, and the
Bryce Report. I have not altered anything, though if it were
written now some alterations would be required. It was to have
appeared in the Italian review, *Scientia*, in June, and was already
in proof, but was withdrawn in consequence of Italy's joining
in the war. It appeared, with some omissions, in Nos. 4 and 5
of the Swiss *International Review*.

To this attitude there have been notable exceptions
among literary men—for example, Romain Rolland
and Bernard Shaw—and even among politicians,
although political extinction is now everywhere the
penalty for a sense of justice. Among men of learning, there are no doubt many who have preserved
justice in their thoughts and in their private utterances. But these men, whether from fear or from unwillingness to seem unpatriotic, have almost kept
silence. Among those who have published their opinions, almost all have shown a complete lack of intellectual detachment. Such an article as that of V.
Pareto in *Scientia* could hardly have been written by
a professor in one of the belligerent countries.*

I cannot but think that the men of learning, by
allowing partiality to colour their thoughts and words,
have missed the opportunity of performing a service
to mankind for which their training should have spe-
cially fitted them. The truth, whatever it may be, is
the same in England, France, and Germany, in Russia
and in Austria. It will not adapt itself to national
needs: it is in its essence neutral. It stands outside
the clash of passions and hatreds, revealing, to those
who seek it, the tragic irony of strife with its attendant
world of illusions. Men of learning, who should be
accustomed to the pursuit of truth in their daily work,
might have attempted, at this time, to make themselves
the mouthpiece of truth, to see what was false on their
own side, what was valid on the side of their enemies.
They might have used their reputation and their

---

*Though the article of N. Kostyleff in the April number of
*Scientia* falls not far short of a completely just outlook.

freedom from political entanglements to mitigate the abhorrence with which the nations have come to regard each other, to help towards mutual understanding, to make the peace, when it comes, not a mere cessation due to weariness, but a fraternal reconciliation, springing from realisation that the strife has been a folly of blindness. They have chosen to do nothing of all this. Allegiance to country has swept away allegiance to truth. Thought has become the slave of instinct, not its master. The guardians of the temple of Truth have betrayed it to idolaters, and have been the first to promote the idolatrous worship.

One of the most surprising things in this war is the universal appeal to atavistic moral notions which, in times of peace, civilised men would have repudiated with contempt. Germans speak of England's brutal national egotism, and represent Germany as fighting to maintain a great ideal of civilisation against an envious world. Englishmen speak of Germany's ruthless militarism and lust of dominion, and represent themselves as fighting to uphold the sacredness of treaties and the rights of small nations. In a sober mood, many of the men who use such language would recognise that it is melodramatic and mythical. All nations, at all times, are egotistic. It may happen, accidentally, that in pursuing its own interest a nation is also spreading civilisation or upholding the sacredness of treaties; but no impartial person can believe that for such ends a nation will sacrifice a million lives and a thousand millions of pounds. Such sacrifices are only made for nationally selfish ends, and until it is recognised that all the nations engaged in the war are equally and wholly selfish, no true thought about the issues involved is possible.

Moral judgments, as applied to others than oneself, are a somewhat subtilised police force: they make use of men's desire for approbation to bring self-interest into harmony with the interest of one's neighbours. But when a man is already trying to kill you, you will not feel much additional discomfort in the thought that he has a low opinion of your moral character. For this reason, disapproval of our enemies in war-time is useless, so far as any possible effect upon them is concerned. It has, however, a certain unconscious purpose, which is, to prevent humane feelings towards the enemy, and to nip in the bud any nascent sympathy for his sufferings. Under the stress of danger, beliefs and emotions all become subservient to the one end of self-preservation. Since it is repugnant to civilised men to kill and maim others just like themselves, it becomes necessary to conquer repugnance by denying the likeness and imputing wickedness to those whom we wish to injure. And so it comes about that the harshest moral judgments of the enemy are formed by the nations which have the strongest impulses of kindliness to overcome.

In order to support this belief in the peculiar wickedness of the enemy, a whole mythology of falsehood grows up, partly through the deliberate action of newspapers and governments, but chiefly through the inherent myth-making tendency of strong collective emotions. Every powerful passion brings with it an impulse to an attendant system of false beliefs. A man in love will attribute innumerable non-existent

perfections to the object of his devotion; a jealous man
will attribute equally non-existent crimes to the object
of his jealousy. But in ordinary life, this tendency is
continually held in check by intercourse with people
who do not share our private passions, and who therefore are critical of our irrational beliefs. In national
questions, this corrective is absent. Most men meet
few foreigners, especially in time of war, and beliefs
inspired by passion can be communicated to others
without fear of an unsympathetic response. The supposed facts intensify the passion which they embody,
and are magnified still further by those to whom they
are told. Individual passions, except in lunatics,
produce only the germs of myths, perpetually neutral-
ised by the indifference of others; but collective passions escape this corrective, and generate in time what
appears like overwhelming evidence for wholly false
beliefs.

Men of learning, who are acquainted with the part
played by collective error in the history of religion,
ought to have been on their guard against assaults
upon their credulity. They ought to have realised,
from the obvious falsehood of the correlative opposite
beliefs in enemy countries, that the myth-making impulse was unusually active, and could only be repelled
by an unusual intellectual vigour. But I do not find
that they were appreciably less credulous than the
multitude. In the early days of last September, when
the Germans were carrying all before them in France,
the need for some source of hope produced in England
an all but universal belief that a large Russian army
had travelled from Archangel, through England, to

Belgium. The evidence was very much better than the evidence for most facts of history: most men knew many eye-witnesses of their transit, and at last a newspaper published a telegram from its correspondent saying that he had discovered them in Belgium. Only then was the story officially denied, but for a long time many continued to believe it. And the intellectuals were not by any means less ready to believe it than the rest of the country.

The really harmful beliefs are those which produce hatred of the enemy. The devastation and maltreatment of Belgium might naturally have aroused some qualms among humane Germans. But the instinct of self-protection produced a harvest of accusations against the Belgians: that they put out the eyes of wounded Germans, or cut off their hands; that they behaved brutally to German women in Belgium; and, generally, that they had shown such depravity as rendered them unworthy of consideration. At the very same time, innumerable German atrocities were reported in England. It cannot, unfortunately, be denied that many very shocking atrocities occurred, but not nearly so many as the English at first believed. Many men stated confidently that they knew people in England who had staying with them Belgian children whose hands had been cut off by German soldiers. Some such cases there were in Belgium, but I know of no evidence that any reached England. No effect whatever was produced by pointing out that if there were so many cases, at least one with a name and address would have been mentioned in the newspaper. Such arguments have no power against a belief which stimulates ferocity, and is on that account felt to be useful. No doubt atrocities have occurred on both sides. But it is certain that they have been far less numerous, and (for the most part) less unnatural, than they are almost universally believed to have been.

A correspondence in the *Labour Leader* for March 18 will illustrate this point.

Rev. J. F. Matthews,
Glossop Road Baptist Church,
        Sheffield.

DEAR SIR,

A correspondent informs us that on Sunday morning you stated in the course of a sermon delivered in Wash Lane Church, Latchford, Warrington, that there is a Belgian girl in Sheffield with her nose cut off and her stomach ripped open by the Germans, and that she is still living and getting better.

I am anxious to investigate stories of German atrocities, and should be grateful if you could send particulars to me by which your statements could be authenticated.

Faithfully yours,
*March 5, 1915.*                    A. FENNER BROCKWAY.

Mr. A. Fenner Brockway.

DEAR SIR,

Thank you for your note. I have written to our Belgian Consul here for the name and address of the girl whose case I quoted at Latchford. If all I hear is true it is far worse than I stated. I am also asking for another similar instance, which I shall be glad to transmit to you if, and as soon as, I can secure the facts.

I am, yours very sincerely,
*March 9, 1915.*                    JOHN FRANCIS MATTHEWS.

DEAR MR. BROCKWAY,

I enclose our Consul's letter, which I have just received. I am writing a letter to my old Church at Latchford, to be read on Sunday next, contradicting the story which I told, on what seemed to be unimpeachable authority. I am glad I did not give the whole of the alleged facts as they were given to me. With many thanks for your note and inquiry.

I am, yours sincerely,
*March 12, 1915.*                    JOHN FRANCIS MATTHEWS.

DEAR MR. MATTHEWS,

Replying to your letter of the 9th inst., enclosing a letter which you have received from the *Labour Leader*, although I have heard of a number of cases of Belgian girls being maltreated in one way and another, I have on investigation not found a particle of truth in one of them, and I know of no girl in Sheffield who has had her nose cut off and her stomach ripped open.

I have also investigated cases in other towns, but have not yet succeeded in getting hold of any tangible confirmation.

Yours very truly,

A. BALFAY,

(Belgian Consul at Sheffield).

*March 11, 1915.*

I have not the means of giving similar illustrations of false beliefs in Germany and Austria. But in case this book should be read by any German or Austrian, I would beg him not to infer any peculiar English credulity, but to realise that such false stories are an accident of war, and that a great deal of what the German or Austrian public believes on apparently unimpeachable evidence is sure to be untrue. No man with any spark of justice in his nature will *deliberately* wish to think worse of his enemies than they deserve. So long as he is not on his guard, his instinct will play tricks with his judgment. We all perceive quite easily that this happens in enemy nations; what I wish to point out is that it happens in *all* the belligerent nations. Those who remark pityingly that the enemy are deluded with lies ought to remember our common human nature, and to realise that their own nation is equally deluded with exactly similar "lies" —though "lies" is hardly the word, since there is very little deliberate deception involved.

There is, however, another class of false beliefs, in which deliberate deception has played a greater part. These are false beliefs on political matters of fact. I will give two illustrations, one on each side.

In Germany, the belief seems to be almost universal that England violated the neutrality of Belgium before Germany did so. This belief is based partly on the assertion that the English sent troops to Belgium before the declaration of war, partly on the military conversations in Brussels in 1906 and 1912. As to the first of these allegations, not only has it been denied by our Government, which Germans could hardly be expected to regard as evidence; not only is its falsehood evident from the Belgian Grey Book, which Germans might regard as a piece of skillful manipulation; not only are those among us who have many acquaintances in the Army, and who must have heard privately if any troops were sent abroad, able to assert with absolute certainty that no such event took place; but the military events of last August are sufficient proof, one would have supposed, even to the credulity of an enemy. No English prisoners were taken by the Germans in their early battles with Belgians, and so far as I have heard they do not even allege that they encountered any English before they reached Mons.

The assertion that the military conversations constituted a breach of neutrality is supported by omitting the fact that all the arrangements were conditional upon the Germans first invading Belgium. It was well known that this was likely to happen in the event of war, and that England and France would, in that case, attempt the defence of Belgium if possible. If, when the time came, the Germans had respected Belgian neutrality, they might have pointed to the conversations as proof of groundless suspicion. But in view of what has occurred, it is absurd to pretend that England and Belgium had no right to consider in common how they should meet a threatening danger which proves to have been only too real. The German accusation, like the charges of atrocities brought against Belgians, is merely a symptom of a bad conscience, not an outcome of any calm consideration of the evidence.

My other illustration concerns the dates of mobilisation. It is usually asserted in England that Austria's general mobilisation preceded Russia's, whereas the opposite seems almost certainly the truth. At the time, the true view was generally accepted in England, just as Bethmann-Hollweg admitted that the invasion of Belgium was a wrong. But just as this admission was seen to constitute a fatal weakness in Germany's pose, so the Russian mobilisation was seen to constitute a weakness in the Allies' contention that Germany deliberately planned the war. And so each side set to work to explain away its earlier admissions, and to produce a completely comfortable state of mind by methods which seem hard to acquit wholly of deliberate falsification. But on neither side have the intellectuals made any appreciable attempt to resist the process of self-deception to which their Governments invited them. What little attempt at truth there has been has been almost wholly confined to Socialists, who had none of the educational advantages which proved so unavailing among professors.

The beliefs which the learned have allowed themselves to share with their compatriots are not only independent of fact in their broad outlines, but are inspired, even in their niceties, by the instincts connected with combat. The Germans have strong hope of a separate peace with France, some hope of a separate peace with Russia, and no hope of a separate peace with England. It follows from this that the French are not wicked at all, the Russians are only moderately wicked, while the English are a blot upon the human race. The English feel quite certain that the Allies can crush the Turks, fairly confident that they can prevent the Austrians from ever again becoming a danger, but not all sure that they can break the spirit of Germany. They deduce that the Turks are brave misguided, the Austrians the mere tools of Prussia, while the Germans deserve to be condemned to the lowest pit of hell. It is useless to urge that the Turks have been for ages a by-word of cruelty, that the Austrians have *primâ facie* more responsibility for the war than the Germans, or that the Germans have contributed much of what is most valuable in the civilisation of the world. Such mere facts carry no weight: moral reprobation is nothing but an embodiment of hatred, and hatred is a mechanical product of biological instinct. It is unworthy of men who pretend to freedom of thought to be caught in the toils of this purely animal mechanism. There is no reason to expect an unusual degree of humane feeling from professors; but some pride of rationality, some unwillingness to let judgment be enslaved by brutal passions, we might have hoped to find. But we should have hoped in vain.

The fundamental irrational belief, on which all the others rest, is the belief that the victory of one's own side is of enormous and indubitable importance, and even of such importance as to outweigh all the evils involved in prolonging the war. It is possible, in view of the uncertainty of all human affairs, that the victory of one side or the other might bring great good to humanity. But even if this be the case, the beliefs of the combatants are none the less irrational, since there is no evidence such as would convince an impartial outsider. The Allies are convinced that their victory is for the good of mankind, and the Germans and Austrians are no less convinced in the opposite sense. When a large mass of men hold one opinion, and another large mass hold another, and when in each case the opinion is in accordance with self-interest, it is hardly to be supposed that it is based on rational grounds either on the one side or on the other. Meanwhile the evils produced by the war increase from day to day, and they, at least, must be admitted by both sides equally.

The difference of opinion as to the desirable issue of the war is not wholly due to self-interest, though that is no doubt the chief cause. The difference is due in part to divergent ideals embodying divergent desires. Putting the matter crudely, and considering only the Western war, we may say that the Germans love order, learning, and music, all of which are good things, while the French and English love democracy and liberty, which are also good things. In order to force their respective ideals upon nations which do not value them, the Germans are willing to replace order in Europe by the universal chaos of war, and to send the young men who pursue learning or music to be killed on the battlefield, while the French and English have found it necessary to suppress democracy and liberty for the present, without any guarantee that they will be restored when the war is over. If the war lasts long, all that was good in the ideals of Germany, France, and England will have perished, as the ideals of Spartans and Athenians perished in the Peloponnesian War. All three races, with all that they have added to our civilisation, will have become exhausted, and victory, when it comes, will be as barren and as hopeless as defeat.

Under the distorting influence of war, the doubtful and microscopic differences between different European nations have been exaggerated when it has become treason to question their overwhelming importance. Every educated man knew and acknowledged before the war began, and every educated man now knows without acknowledging, that the likenesses among European nations are immeasurably greater than their differences. Congresses, conferences, and international bodies of many kinds testified to the diffused consciousness of a common purpose, a common task in the life of civilisation. Suddenly, between one day and the next, all this is forgotten: German scholars repudiate English honours, English scholars say that Germany has done nothing of importance in learning. In a moment, all the great co-operative work for which academic bodies exist is set aside for the pleasure of indulging a bitter and trivial hatred.

This war is trivial, for all its vastness. No great principle is at stake, no great human purpose is involved on either side. The supposed ideal ends for which it is being fought are merely part of the myth. Every nation is fighting in self-defence, every nation is fighting to destroy the tyranny of armaments, every nation is fighting to show that unprovoked aggression cannot be practised with impunity. Every nation pays homage to peace by maintaining that its enemies began the war. The fact that these assertions carry equal conviction on both sides shows that they are not based on reason, but are merely inspired by prejudice. But besides these common objects, there are some in which the two sides differ. Probably the two Kaisers would say, and perhaps believe, that they are fighting to prove it a crime to assassinate heirs to thrones. It can hardly be supposed that the Tsar would deny that this is a crime, but he would say, as the English do, that it is a crime for a great nation to oppress a small one. This proposition, however, is only true in certain latitudes; it does not apply to Finland or Persia. The English and French say they are fighting in defence of democracy, but they do not wish their words to be heard in Petrograd or Calcutta. And, oddly enough, those who most bitterly hate democracy at home are the most ferocious in defending it against Germany.

This war is not being fought for any rational end: it is being fought because, at first, the nations wished to fight, and now they are angry and determined to win victory. Everything else is idle talk, artificial rationalising of instinctive actions and passions. When two dogs fight in the street, no one supposes that anything but instinct prompts them, or that they are inspired by high and noble ends. But if they were capable of what is called thought, if they had been taught that Dog is a rational animal, we may be sure that a superstructure of belief would grow up in them during the combat. They fight really because something angers them in each other's smell. But if their fighting were accompanied by intellectual activity, the one would say he was fighting to promote the right kind of smell (*Kulter*), and the other to uphold the inherent canine right of running on the pavement (democracy). Yet this would not prevent the bystanders from seeing that their action was foolish, and that they ought to be parted as soon as possible. And what is true of dogs in the street is equally true of nations in the present war.

The original impulse towards war, though by now it has spent its force, was very strong in the first days. Fighting and killing are among the natural activities of males, both of human beings and of the higher animals. The spectacle of males killing each other in sexual combat is pleasant, presumably, to animal females, and certainly to many of those of the species *homo sapiens*. Owing to the activities of the police, opportunities for these pleasures are much curtailed in civilised countries. For this reason, when war is coming there is a liberation of a whole set of instinctive activities normally repressed. This brings with it an exhilaration comparable to that of falling in love. Instead of being oppressed by the prospect of the horrors of war—friends and relations killed or maimed, countries ravaged, civilisation bleeding in the mire—most men, in the first days, were excited and happy, feeling an unusual freedom, and inventing, with unconscious hypocrisy, all sorts of humane reasons to excuse their joy. In this mood there is no great hatred of the enemy: he has his uses, since without him there could be no fighting. The injury to him is a merely incidental and almost regrettable result of the battle. Primitive poetry is full of this mood, and the early days of August showed that it is still possible to civilised men.

But when, as in this war, neither side wins decisive successes, and the utmost effort is required to avert disaster, the honeymoon intoxication of the first moments is soon succeeded by a sterner mood. Checks cause fury, and injuries suffered produce hatred. More and more men's thought become concentrated on humbling the pride of their enemies. If the war remains undecided for a long time, if the new levies on both sides are exterminated without either victory or defeat, there will be a growing ferocity, leading to horrors such as even this war has not yet brought into the imaginations of men. One by one soldiers will pass suddenly from ferocity to apathy: the spring of will will break, leaving millions of derelicts fit only for the hospital or the asylum. This is what the German military authorities mean when they say that the war will be decided by nervous endurance. They hope that a smaller percentage of the Germans than of the Allies will be broken by the strain. Militarists on both sides look forward cheerfully to the extinction, for all purposes of national life, of most of the men now between twenty and forty. And yet they continue to pretend that the victory of their side is more important than an early peace. And in this infamy

their professorial parasites support them and egg
them on.

The worst disasters would have been averted if
either side had won a rapid victory, and are even now
not inevitable if the war comes to an end during this
year. But if peace is not made soon, if no military
decision is reached, there will have to be an increasing
passionate concentration of will in all countries upon
the one common purpose of mutual destruction. As
the effort of will required grows greater and more
difficult through weariness, the vital force of the
nations will be more and more weakened. When at
last peace comes, it is to be feared that no stimulus
will be adequate to rouse men to action. After the
fierce tension of combat, nothing will seem important;
a weak and relaxed dissipation will succeed the terrible unnatural concentration. There is no parallel
in history to the conflict in which the world is now
engaged. Never before have so large a proportion of
the population been engaged in fighting, and never
before has the fighting been so murderous. All that
science and organisation have done to increase the
efficiency of labour has been utilised to set free more
men for the destructive work of the battlefield. Man's
greater command over Nature has only magnified the
disaster, because it has not been accomplished by geater
command over his own passions. And if he does
not acquire command over his own passions, whatever destruction is not achieved now is only postponed
to a later day.

The degradation of science from its high function in
ameliorating the lot of man is one of the most painful

aspects of this war. Savage man, like the brutes, lives
in bondage to matter: the task of securing a bare
subsistence absorbs his energies, leaving no leisure for
art and thought and the goods of the mind. From this
bondage science has been progressively liberating the
populations of civilized countries. One man's labour
now will produce a great deal more than one man's
food. Out of the time set free in this way have grown
literature and music, poetry and philosophy, and the
intoxicating triumphs of science itself. On the basis
of the greater productivity of labour, education,
democracy, and all the political advances of the modern
State have been built. Suddenly, now, because a
madness of destruction has swept over Europe, the
men of science have abandoned their beneficent
activities: physicists invent swifter aircraft, chemists
devise more deadly explosives, and almost all who can,
devote themselves to the labour of death. The place
of science in human development, one is compelled to
think, has never become present to their minds, since
they are willing to prostitute it to the undoing of its
own work.

Knowledge with elevation of mind is the chief
instrument of human progress; knowledge without
elevation of mind easily becomes devilish, and increases
the wounds which man inflicts on man. Men of
learning should be the guardians of one of the sacred
fires that illumine the darkness into which the human
spirit is born: upon them depends the ideal of just
thought, of disinterested pursuit of truth, which, if it
had existed more widely, would have sufficed alone to
prevent the present horror. To serve this ideal, to

keep alive a purpose remote from strife, is more worthy
of the intellectual leaders of Europe than to help
Governments in stimulating hatred or slaughtering
more of the young men upon whom the future of the
world depends.    It is time to forget our supposed
separate duty toward Germany, Austria, Russia,
France, or England, and remember that higher duty
to mankind in which we can still be at one.

# THE ETHICS OF WAR.*

THE question whether war is ever justified, and if so under what circumstances, is one which has been forcing itself upon the attention of all thoughtful men. It seems to me that no single one of the combatants is justified in the present war, and yet I cannot believe that war is under all circumstances a crime. Opinions on such a subject as war are the outcome of feeling rather than of thought: given a man's emotional temperament, his convictions, both on war in general and on any particular war which may occur during his lifetime can be predicted with tolerable certainty. The arguments used will merely reinforce what comes out of a man's nature. The fundamental facts in this as in all ethical questions are feelings; all that thought can do is to clarify and harmonise the expression of those feelings, and it is such clarifying and harmonising of my own feelings that I wish to attempt in the present article.

## I.

The question of the rights and wrongs of a particular war is generally considered from a juridical or quasi-juridical standpoint: A certain country broke a certain treaty, crossed a certain frontier, committed certain technically unfriendly acts, and, therefore, by the rules, it is permissible to kill as many of the soldiers of that country as modern armaments render

*Reprinted from the *International Journal of Ethics*, January, 1915.

possible. There is a certain unreality, a certain lack of imaginative grasp about this way of viewing matters. It has the advantage, always dearly prized by lazy men, of substituting a formula, at once ambiguous and easily applied, for the vital realisation of the consequences of acts. The judicial point of view is properly applicable to the relations of individuals within a State, but not, as yet, to the relations between States. Within a State, private war is forbidden, and the disputes of private citizens are settled, not by their own force, but by the force of the police, which, being overwhelming, very seldom needs to be explicity displayed. There have to be rules according to which the police decide, who is to be considered in the right in a private dispute, and these rules constitute law. The chief gain derived from the law and the police is the abolition of private wars, and this gain is secured even if the law as it stands is not the best possible. It is therefore in the public interest that the man who goes against the law should be considered in the wrong, not because of the excellence of the law, but because of the importance of preventing individuals within the State from resorting to force.

In the interrelations of States nothing of the same sort exists. There is, it is true, a body of conventions called "international law," and there are innumerable treaties between High Contracting Powers. But the conventions and the treaties differ from anything that could properly be called law by the absence of sanction: there is no police force able or willing to enforce their observance. It follows from this that every nation concludes multitudes of divergent and incompatible treaties, and that, in spite of the high language one sometimes hears, the main purpose of the treaties is in actual fact to afford the sort of pretext which is considered respectable for engaging in war with another Power. A Great Power is considered unscrupulous when it goes to war without previously providing itself with such a pretext—unless, indeed, its opponent is a small country, in which case it is only to be blamed if that small country happens to be under the protection of some other Great Power. England and Russia may partition Persia immediately after guaranteeing its integrity and independence, because no other Great Power has a recognised interest in Persia, and Persia is one of those small States in regard to which treaty obligations are not considered binding. France and Spain, under a similar guarantee to Morocco, must not partition it without first compensating Germany, because it is recognised that, until such compensation has been offered and accepted, Germany, though not Morocco, has a legitimate interest in the preservation of that country. All Great Powers having guaranteed the neutrality of Belgium, England has a recognised right to resent its violation—a right which is exercised when it is believed to be to England's interest, and waived when England's interest is not thought to be involved. A treaty is therefore not to be regarded as a contract having the same kind of binding force as belongs to private contracts; it is to be regarded only as a means of giving notice to rival Powers that certain acts may, if the national interest so demand, form one of those reasons for war which are recognised as legitimate. If the faithful observance of treaties were a frequent occurrence, like the observance of contracts, the breach of a treaty might be a real and not merely a formal ground for war, since it would tend to weaken the practice of deciding disputes by agreement rather than by armed force. In the absence of such a practice, however, appeal to treaties is only to be regarded as part of the diplomatic machinery. A nation whose diplomacy has been skilfully conducted will always be able to find some treaty or agreement bringing its intervention within the rules of the diplomatic game when it believes that its interests demand war. But so long as treaties are only observed when it is convenient to do so, the rules of the diplomatic game have nothing to do with the question whether embarking or participating in a war will or will not be for the good of mankind, and it is this question which has to be decided in considering whether a war is justified or not.

## II.

It is necessary, in regard to any war, to consider not its paper justification in past agreements, but its real justification in the balance of good which it is to bring to mankind. At the beginning of a war each nation, under the influence of what is called patriotism, believes that its own victory is both certain and of great importance to mankind. The praiseworthiness of this belief has become an accepted maxim: even when war is actually in progress it is held to be natural and right that a citizen of an enemy country should regard the victory of his side as assured and highly desirable. By concentrating attention upon the supposed advantages of the victory of our own side, we become more or less blind to the evils inseparable from war and equally certain whichever side may ultimately prove victorious. Yet so long as these are not fully realised, it is impossible to judge justly whether a war is or is not likely to be beneficial to the human race. Although the theme is trite, it is necessary briefly to remind ourselves what the evils of war really are.

To begin with the most obvious evil: large numbers of young men, the most courageous and the most physically fit in their respective nations, are killed, bringing great sorrow to their friends, loss to the community, and gain only to themselves, since they escape the horror of existence in this world of strife. Many others are maimed for life, some go mad, and others become nervous wrecks, mere useless and helpless derelicts. Of those who survive many will be brutalised and morally degraded by the fierce business of killing, which, however much it may be the soldier's duty, must shock and often destroy the most humane instincts. As every truthful record of war shows, fear and hate let loose the wild beast in a certain proportion of combatants, leading to strange cruelties, which must be faced, but not dwelt upon if sanity is to be preserved.

Of the evils of war to the non-combatant population in the regions where fighting occurs, the recent misfortunes of Belgium have afforded an example upon which it is not necessary to enlarge. It *is* necessary, however, to combat the common belief of English people that the misfortunes of Belgium afford a reason in favour of war. By a tragic delusion, hatred perpetuates the evils from which it springs. The sufferings of Belgium are attributed to the Germans, not to war, and thus the very horrors of the war are used to make men desire to increase their area and intensity. Even assuming the utmost possible humanity in the conduct of military operations, it cannot be doubted that if the troops of the Allies penetrate into the industrial regions of Germany, the German population will have to suffer a great part of the misfortunes which Germany has inflicted upon Belgium. To men under the influence of hate this thought is a cause of rejoicing, but to men in whom humane feeling is not extinct it shows that our sympathy with Belgium should make us hate war rather than Germany.

The evils which war produces outside the area of military operations are perhaps even more serious, for, though less intense, they are far more widespread. Passing by the anxiety and sorrow of those whose sons or husbands or brothers are at the front, the extent and consequences of the economic injury inflicted by war are much greater than is usually realised. It is common to speak of economic evils as merely material, and of desire for economic progress as grovelling and uninspired. This view is perhaps natural in well-to-do people, to whom economic progress means setting up a motor car or taking holidays abroad instead of at the seaside. But with regard to the poorer classes of society, economic progress is the first condition of many spiritual goods, and even often of life itself. An overcrowded family, living in a slum in conditions of filth and immorality, where half the children die from ignorance of hygiene and bad sanitation, and the remainder grow up stunted and ignorant—such a family can hardly make progress mentally or spiritually, except through an improvement in its economic condition.  And without going to the very bottom of the social scale, economic progress is necessary for a good education, for a tolerable existence for women, and for that breadth and freedom of outlook upon which **any solid and national advance** must be based. It is not the most oppressed or the most ill-used who make an effective plea for social justice, for some reorganization of society which shall give less to the idler and more to the common man.  Throughout the Napoleonic wars, while the landowners of England continually increased their rent-rolls, the mass of the wage-earning population sank into greater and greater destitution.  It was only afterwards, during the long peace, that a less unjust distribution began to be possible.  It cannot be doubted that the desire on the part of the rich to distract men's minds from the claims of social justice has been more or less unconsciously one of the motives leading to war in modern Europe.  Everywhere the well-to-do, and the political parties which represent their interests, have been the chief agents in stirring up international hatred and in persuading the working man that his real enemy is the foreigner.  Thus war, and the fear of war, has a double effect in retarding social progress : it diminishes the resources available for improving the condition of the wage-earning classes, and it distracts men's minds from the need and possibility of general improvement by persuading them that the way to better themselves is to injure their comrades in some other country. It is as a protest against this delusion that international Socialism has arisen; and whatever may be the thought of Socialism as an economic doctrine, its internationalism makes it the sanest force in modern politics, and the only large body which has preserved some degrees of judgment and humanity in the present chaos.

But of all the evils of war the greatest is the purely spiritual evil: the hatred, the injustice, the repudiation of truth, the artificial conflict, where, if the nations could once overcome the blindness of inherited instincts and the sinister influence of anti-social interests, such as those of armaments with their subservient press, it would be seen that there is a real consonance of interest and essential identity of human nature, and every reason to replace hatred by love. Mr. Norman Angell has well shown how unreal, as applied to the conflicts of civilised States, is the whole vocabulary of international conflict, how illusory are the gains supposed to be obtained by victory, and how fallacious are the injuries which nations, in times of peace, are supposed to inflict upon each other in economic competition. The importance of this thesis lies not so much in its direct economic application as in the hope which it affords for the liberation of better spiritual impulses in the relations of different communities. To love our enemies, however desirable, is not easy, and therefore, it is well to realise that the enmity springs only from blindness, not from any inexorable physical necessity.

### III.

Are there any wars which achieve so much for the good of mankind as to outweigh all the evils we have been considering? I think there have been such wars in the past, but they are not wars of the sort with which our diplomatists are concerned, for which our armies and navies have been prepared, and which are exemplified by the present conflict. For purposes of classification we may roughly distinguish four kinds of wars, though, of course, in any given case a war is not likely to be quite clearly of any one of the four kinds. With this proviso we may distinguish: (1) Wars of Colonisation; (2) Wars of Principle; (3) Wars of Self-defence; (4) Wars of Prestige. Of these four kinds I should say that the first and second are fairly often justified; the third seldom, except as against an adversary of inferior civilisation; and the fourth, which is the sort to which the present war belongs, never. Let us consider these four kinds of war in succession.

By a "war of colonisation" I mean a war whose purpose is to drive out the whole population of some territory and replace it by an invading population of a different race. Ancient wars were very largely of this kind, of which we have a good example in the Book of Joshua. In modern times the conflicts of Europeans with American-Indians, Maories, and other aborigines in temperate regions, have been of this kind. Such wars are totally devoid of *technical* justification, and are apt to be more ruthless than any other war. Nevertheless, if we are to judge by results, we cannot regret that such wars have taken place. They have the merit, often quite fallaciously claimed for all wars, of leading in the main to the survival of the fittest, and it is chiefly through such wars that the civilised portion of the world has been extended from the neighbourhood of the Mediterranean to the greater part of the earth's surface. The eighteenth century, which liked to praise the virtues of the savage and contrast them with the gilded corruption of courts, nevertheless had no scruple in thrusting the noble savage out from his North-American hunting grounds. And we cannot at this date bring ourselves to condemn the process by which the American continent has been acquired for European civilisation. In order that such wars may be justified, it is necessary that there should be a very great and undeniable difference between the civilisation of the colonisers and that of the dispossessed natives. It is necessary, also, that the climate should be one in which the invading race can flourish. When these conditions are satisfied the conquest becomes justified, though actual fighting against the dispossessed inhabitants ought, of course, to be avoided as far as is compatible with colonising. Many humane people will object in theory to the justification of this form of robbery, but I do not think that any practical or effective objection is likely to be made.

Such wars, however, belong now to the past. The regions where the white man live are all allotted, either to white races or to yellow races to whom the white man is not clearly superior, and whom, in any case, he is not strong enough to expel. Apart from small punitive expeditions, wars of colonisation, in the true sense, are no longer possible. What are nowadays called colonial wars do not aim at the complete occupation of a country by a conquering race; they aim only at securing certain governmental and trading advantages. They belong, in fact, rather with what I call wars of prestige than with wars of colonisation in the old sense. There are, it is true, a few rare exceptions. The Greeks in the second Balkan war conducted a war of colonisation against the Bulgarians; throughout a certain territory which they intended to occupy they killed all the men, and carried off all the women. But in such cases the only possible justification fails, since there is no evidence of superior civilisation on the side of the conquerors.

In spite of the fact that wars of colonisation belong to the past, men's feelings and beliefs about war are still those appropriate to the extinct conditions which rendered such wars possible. When the present war began, many people in England imagined that if the Allies were victorious Germany would cease to exist: Germany was to be ''destroyed'' or ''smashed,'' and since these phrases sounded vigorous and cheering, people failed to see that they were totally devoid of meaning. There are some seventy million Germans; with great good fortune we might, in a successful war, succeed in killing two millions of them. There would then still be sixty-eight million Germans, and in a few years the loss of the population due to the war would be made good. Germany is not merely a State, but a nation, bound together by a common language, common traditions, and common ideals. Whatever the outcome of the war, this nation will still exist at the end of it, and its strength cannot be permanently impaired. But imagination in what pertains to war is still dominated by Homer and the Old Testament; men who cannot see that circumstances have changed since those works were composed are called "practical" men, and are said to be free from illusions, while those who have some understanding of the modern world, and some capacity for freeing their minds from the influence of phrases, are called dreamy idealists, Utopians, traitors, and friends of every country but their own. If the facts were understood, wars amongst civilised nations would cease owing to their inherent absurdity. Men's passions always lag behind their political organisation, and facts which leave no outlet for passions are not readily admitted. In order that hatred, pride, and violence may find an outlet, men unconsciously blind themselves to the plainest facts of politics and economics, and modern war continues to be waged with the phrases and theories invented by simpler men in a simpler age.

### IV.

The second type of war which may sometimes be justified is what may be called "the war of principle." To this kind belong the wars of Protestant and Catholic, and the English and American civil wars. In such cases, each side, or at least one side, is honestly convinced that the progress of mankind depends upon the adoption of certain beliefs or institutions, which, through blindness or natural depravity, the other side will not regard as reasonable, except when presented at the point of the bayonet. Such wars may be justi-

fied; for example, a nation practising religious toleration may be justified in resisting a persecuting nation
holding a different creed.  On this ground we might
justify the resistance of the Dutch to the English and
French combined in the time of Charles II.  But wars
of principle are much less often justified than is believed by those in whose age they occur.  It is very
seldom that a principle of genuine value to mankind
can only be propagated by military force: as a rule,
it is the bad part of men's principles, not the good
part, which makes it necessary to fight for their defence.  And for this reason the bad part rather than
the good rises to prominence during the progress of
the war of principle.  A nation undertaking a war in
defence of religious toleration would be almost certain
to persecute those of its citizens who did not believe in
religious toleration.  A war on behalf of democracy,
if it is long and fierce, is sure to end in the exclusion
from all share of power of those who do not support
the war.  Mr. George Trevelyan in an eloquent passage
describes the defeat which, as the ultimate outcome
of our civil war, overtook alike the ideals of the Round-
heads and the ideals of the Cavaliers.  "And this was
the curse of the victors, not to die, but to live, and
almost to lose their awful faith in God, when they saw
the Restoration, not of the old gaiety that was too
gay for them, and the old loyalty that was too loyal
for them, but of corruption and selfishness that had
neither country nor king.  The sound of the Round-
head cannon has long ago died away, but still the
silence of the garden is heavy with unalterable fate,
brooding over besiegers and besieged, in such haste to

destroy each other and permit only the vile to survive.''* This common doom of opposite ideals is the
usual, though not the invariable, penalty of supporting ideals by force. While it may therefore be conceded that such wars are not invariably to be condemned, we must, nevertheless, scrutinise very scep-
tically the claim of any particular war to be justified
on the ground of the victory which it brings to some
important principle.

There are some who maintain that the present war
is a war in defence of democracy. I do not know
whether this view is adopted by the Tsar, and for the
sake of the stability of the Alliance I sincerely hope
that it is not. I do not, however, desire to dispute the
proposition that democracy in the western nations
would suffer from the victory of Germany. What I do
wish to dispute is the belief not infrequently enter-
tained in England that if the Allies are victorious
democracy can be forced upon a reluctant Germany as
part of the conditions of peace. Men who think thus
have lost sight of the spirit of democracy in worship
of the letter. The Germans have the form of government which they desire, and any other form, imposed
by alien victors, would be less in harmony with the
spirit of democracy, however much it might conform
to the letter. Men do right to desire strongly the victory of ideals which they believe to be important, but
it is almost always a sign of yielding to undue im-
patience when they believe that what is valuable in
their ideals can be furthered by substituting force for

*George M. Trevelyan, *Clio, A Muse, and other Essays, literary
and pedestrian,* London, 1913, pages 26-27.

peaceful persuasion. To advocate democracy by war is only to repeat, on a vaster scale and with far more tragic results, the error of those who have sought it hitherto by the assassin's knife and the bomb of the anarchist.

## V.

The next kind of war to be considered is the war of self-defence. This kind of war is almost universally admitted to be justifiable, and is condemned only by Christ and Tolstoy. The justification of wars of self-defence is very convenient, since so far as I know there has never yet been a war which was not one of self-defence. Every strategist assures us that the true defence is offence; every great nation believes that its own overwhelming strength is the only possible guarantee of the world's peace and can only be secured by the defeat of other nations. In the present war, Servia is defending itself against the brutal aggression of Austria-Hungary; Austria-Hungary is defending itself against the disruptive revolutionary agitation which Servia is believed to have fomented; Russia is defending Slavdom against the menace of Teutonic aggression; Germany is defending Teutonic civilisation against the encroachments of the Slav; France is defending itself against a repetition of 1870; and England, which sought only the preservation of the *status quo,* is defending itself against a prospective menace to its maritime supremacy. The claim on each side to be fighting in self-defence appears to the other side mere wanton hypocrisy, because in each case the other side aims at conquest as the only means of self-defence. So long as the principle of self-defence is recognised as affording always a sufficient justification for war, this tragic conflict of irresistible claims remains unavoidable. In certain cases, where there is a clash of differing civilisations, a war of self-defence may be justified on the same grounds as a war of principle. But I think that, even as a matter of practical politics, the principle of non-resistance contains an immense measure of wisdom, if only men would have the courage to carry it out. The evils suffered during a hostile invasion are suffered because resistance is offered: the Duchy of Luxenburg, which was not in a position to offer resistance, has escaped the fate of the other regions occupied by hostile troops. What one civilised nation can achieve against another by means of conquest is very much less than is commonly supposed. It is said, both here and in Germany, that each side is fighting for its existence; but this phrase covers a great deal of confusion of thought induced by unreasoning panic. We cannot destroy Germany even by a complete military victory, nor could Germany destroy England even if our navy were sunk and London occupied by the Prussians. English civilisation, the English language, English manufactures would still exist, and as a matter of practical politics it would be totally impossible for Germany to establish a tyranny in this country. If Germans, instead of being resisted by force of arms, had been passively permitted to establish themselves wherever they pleased, the halo of glory and courage surrounding the brutality of military success would have been absent, and public opinion in Germany itself would have rendered any oppression impossible. The history of our own dealings with our colonies affords abundant examples to show that under such circumstances the refusal of self-government is not possible. In a word, it is the means of repelling hostile aggression which make hostile aggression disastrous and which generate the fear by which hostile nations come to think aggression justified. As between civilised nations, nonresistance would seem not only a distant religious ideal, but the course of practical wisdom. Only pride and fear stand in the way of its adoption. But the pride of military glory might be overcome by a nobler pride, and the fear might be overcome by a clearer realisation of the solidity and indestructibility of a modern civilised nation.

## VI.

The last kind of war we have to consider is what I have called "the war of prestige." Prestige is seldom more than one element in the causes of a war, but it is often a very important element. In the present war, until the war had actually broken out, it was almost the only thing involved, although as soon as the war began other and much more important matters came to be at stake. The initial question between Austria and Russia was almost wholly one of prestige. The lives of Balkan peasants could not have been much affected for good or evil by the participation or non-participation of Austrian officials in the trial of supposed Servian accomplices in the Sarajevo murders. This important question, which is the one on which the war is being fought, concerns what is called the hegemony of the Balkans, and this is entirely a question of prestige. Men desire the sense of triumph, and fear the sense of humiliation which they would have in yielding to the demands of another nation. Rather than forego the triumph, rather than endure the humiliation, they are willing to inflict upon the world all those disasters which it is now suffering and all that exhaustion and impoverishment which it must long continue to suffer. The willingness to inflict and endure such evils is almost universally praised: it is called high-spirited, worthy of a great nation, showing fidelity to ancestral traditions. The slightest sign of reasonableness is attributed to fear, and received with shame on the one side and with derision on the other. In private life exactly the same state of opinion existed so long as duelling was practised, and existed still in those countries in which this custom still survives. It is now recognised, at any rate in the Anglo-Saxon world, that the so-called "honour" which made duelling appear inevitable was a folly and a delusion. It is perhaps not too much to hope that the day may come when the honour of nations, like that of individuals, will be no longer measured by their willingness to inflict slaughter. It can hardly be hoped, however, that such a change will be brought about while the affairs of nations are left in the keeping of diplomats, whose status is bound up with the diplomatic or military triumph of the countries from which they come, and whose manner of life renders them unusually ignorant of all political and economic facts of real importance and of all the changes of opinion and organisation which make the

present world different from that of the eighteenth
century. If any real progress is to be made in intro-
ducing sanity into international relations, these relations must henceforth be in the hands of men less aloof
and less aristocratic, more in touch with common life,
and more emancipated from the prejudices of a by-
gone age. And popular education, instead of inflam-
ing the hatred of foreigners and representing even the
tiniest triumph as worthy of even the greatest sacrifices, must learn to aim rather at producing some sense
of the solidarity of mankind and of the paltryness of
those objects to which diplomatists, often secretly,
think fit to pledge the manhood and heroism of nations.

The objects for which men have fought in the past,
whether just or unjust, are no longer to be achieved
by wars amongst civilised nations. A great weight of
tradition, of financial interests, of political insincerity,
is bound up with the anachronism of war. But it is
perhaps not chimerical to hope that the present war,
which has shocked the conscience of mankind more
than any war in previous history, may produce a re-
vulsion against antiquated methods, and may lead the
exhausted nations to insist upon that brotherhood and
co-operation which their rulers have hitherto denied
them. There is no reason whatever against the settlement of all disputes by a Council of the Powers de-
liberating in public. Nothing stands in its way except
the pride of rulers who wish to remain uncontrolled by
anything higher than their own will. When this great
tragedy has worked itself out to its disastrous conclusion, when the passions of hate and self-assertion have

given place to compassion with the universal misery, the nations will perhaps realise that they have fought in blindness and delusion, and that the way of mercy is the way of happiness for all.

# WAR AND NON-RESISTANCE*

THE principle that it is always wrong to employ force against another human being has been held in its extreme form by Quakers and by Tolstoy, but has always been rejected by the great majority of mankind as inconsistent with the existence of civilised society. In this, no doubt, the majority of mankind are in the right. But I think that the occasions where forcible resistance is the best course are much fewer than is generally believed, and that some very great and important advances in civilisation might be made if this were more widely recognised. The so-called "right of self-defence," in particular, seems to have only a very limited sphere of application, and to be often supported by arguments involving both mistakes as to political questions and a wrong conception of the best type of character.*

No one who holds that human conduct ought to be such as to promote certain ends—no matter what ends may be selected—will expect any absolute hard-and-fast rules of conduct to which no possible exception can be found. Not to lie, not to steal, not to murder, are very good precepts for ordinary cases: it may be, in view of the likelihood of biassed judgments, that most men will act better if they always follow these

*Reprinted from the *Atlantic Monthly*, August, 1915.
I touched upon this subject in a former article, in the *International Journal of Ethics* (January, 1915), but as my discussion was very brief, it was misunderstood, and seems in need of expansion. The present article is a partial reply to Professor Perry in the April Number of that Journal, but I have thought it better to make the reply explanatory rather than controversial.

precepts unquestioningly than if they consider each case on its merits. Nevertheless, it is obvious that there are cases where lying and stealing are justifiable, and the same must be said of murder by those who hold that some wars are righteous. Tolstoy does not judge conduct by its consequences: he considers actions inherently right or wrong. This makes it possible for him to say that no use of force is ever right. But if we judge conduct, as I think we ought, by its power of promoting what we consider a good life or a good society, we cannot expect such simplicity in our moral precepts, and we must expect all of them to be subject to exceptions. Whatever we may have to say must be regarded as in the nature of practical maxims, to be applied with common sense, not as logically universal rules to be tested by extreme cases.*

Broadly speaking, I think the use of force is justifiable when it is ordered in accordance with law by a neutral authority, in the general interest and not primarily in the interest of one of the parties to the quarrel. On this ground, the use of force by the police is justifiable, provided (as is no doubt sometimes the case) the authorities are employing the police in the general interest and not merely in the interest of the holders of power. In international affairs, if there were a Council of the Powers, strong enough to restrain any aggressive nation without great difficulty, any army or navy employed in obedience to its orders might be regarded as a police force, and justified on

---

*Professor Perry (page 311) confronts me with an extreme case. But I had provided for such cases by admitting that a war of self-defence is sometimes a war of principle, and justifiable on that ground.

the same grounds on which the police are justified. I think there is more hope of ultimately achieving universal peace by this method than by the adoption of non-resistance. But this has no bearing upon the question whether non-resistance would be a good policy, if any nation could be induced to adopt it. So long as no Council of the Powers exists, there is no neutral authority to order resistance, and we have to consider the justification of repelling an attack when the nation attacked is the judge in its own cause.

The justification of non-resistance is more easily seen in the case of quarrels between individuals. If I encountered the traditional highwayman, and he demanded my money or my life, I should unhesitatingly give him my money, even if it were in my power to shoot him before he shot me. I should do this, not from cowardice or lack of spirit, but because I would rather part with money than have a man's blood on my conscience. And for the same reason, if I were compelled to engage in a duel, I would rather let my adversary shoot me than shoot him. In this I believe all humane people would agree. At the same time, if he were a worthless fellow, and I had just made an important mathematical discovery which I had not yet had time to record, it might be right to preserve my life at his expense. Arguments of this sort would justify civilised communities in defending themselves against savages. But conflicts between civilised nations are more like conflicts between rival metaphysicians, each of whom considers his own system admirable and the other man's abominable, while to outsiders it is obvious that both are equally fantastic.

In private life, most situations can be met by the double principle of neither employing force nor obeying it. It is a familiar Platonic thesis that the man who inflicts injustice is more to be pitied than the man who suffers it. But such statements are read with a smile, as charming literary paradoxes, and are not taken as practical wisdom for the guidance of life. Yet the use of force to coerce another man's will, even in those rare cases in which it is justifiable, produces a brutal and tyrannous state of mind, and is more destructive of inward peace than any misfortune that can be inflicted from without. The greatest good that can be achieved in this life is to have will and desire directed to universal ends, purged of the self-assertion which belongs to instinctive will. A man who has once known this good will not consider any private end important enough to be fought for: he may be willing to enter upon a contest of force, but if so, it will be for some end outside his own life, since what is best in his own life cannot be taken from him by another. But although he will not dictate to others for his own ends, he will also not be turned aside from universal ends by others: he will be no more willing to obey than to command. He will preserve his own liberty as scrupulously as he respects the liberty of others.

Exactly similar considerations apply to the conduct of nations, but they are obscured by traditional phrases about "honour," "patriotism," " sacred traditions," or "the protection of women and children." It is assumed that a nation which does not oppose force with force must be actuated by cowardice, and must lose whatever is valuable in its civilisation. Both these are illusions. To oppose force by passive non-obedience would require more courage, and would be far more likely to preserve the best elements of the national life. It would also do far more to discourage the use of force. This would be the way of practical wisdom, if men could be brought to believe it. But I fear men are too much wedded to the belief that patriotism is a virtue, and too fond of proving their superiority to others in a contest of force. People who object to the doctrine that might is right always contend that it will be disproved by showing that might is on their own side. Yet that would only be a disproof if their side were in the wrong, and their argument shows that they really believe the doctrine they are pretending to combat. Those who genuinely disbelieve the doctrine will not attempt to disprove it by getting might on their side.

Let us imagine that England were to disband its army and navy, after a generation of instruction in the principles of passive resistance as a better defence than war. Let us suppose that England at the same time publicly announced that no armed opposition would be offered to an invader, that all might come freely, but that no obedience would be yielded to any commands that a foreign authority might issue. What would happen in this case?

Suppose, to continue the argument, that the German Government wished to take advantage of England's defenceless condition. It would be faced, at the outset, by the opposition of whatever was not utterly brutal in Germany, since no possible cloak could be found to hide the nakedness of aggression. All

civilised countries, when they engage in war, find some
decent excuse: they fight, almost always, either in
self-defence or in defence of the weak. No such
excuse could be found in this case. It could no longer
be said, as the Germans now say, that England's
naval preponderance keeps other nations in bondage,
and threatens the very existence of any nation which
depends upon imported food. It could no longer be
said that we were oppressing India, since India would
be able to separate from the British Empire whenever
it wished to do so. All the usual pretexts by which
aggression is justified would be lacking. When
America attacked Spain, it was to liberate the Cubans,
against whom Spain was carrying on a war. When
England attacked the Transvaal, the Poet Laureate,
the *Times*, Messrs. Werner, Beit and Co., and the
other imperialist magnates who represented the
ancient traditions of the British race, solemnly assured
us that our intervention was necessary for the safety
of English women in Johannesburg, and for the liberation of the natives from virtual slavery to the Boers.
These pleas deceived many people who, though no
doubt not unwilling to be deceived, would yet have
shrunk from an aggression which could not be in any
way disguised. And it was said that the Boers aimed
at the conquest of the whole of South Africa: we were
told that, if ever England found itself entangled in a
European war, Cape Colony would be overrun, and its
English colonists would be subjected to a tyranny. In
any civilised country, arguments of this kind are
always used in justifying even the most aggressive
war.

If England had no army and no navy, the Germans would be hard put to it to find a pretext for invasion. All the Liberal elements in Germany would oppose any such enterprise; so would all other nations, unless Germany offered them a share of the plunder. But let us suppose all home opposition overcome, and a force despatched to England to take possession of the country. Such a force, since it would meet with no military opposition, would not need to be large, and would not be in the state of mingled fear and ferocity which characterises an invading army among a hostile population. There would be no difficulty in preserving military discipline, and no opportunity for the rape and rapine which have always been displayed by troops after victory in battle. There would be no glory to be won, not even enough to earn one iron cross. The Germans could not congratulate themselves upon their military prowess, or imagine that they were displaying the stern self-abnegation believed to be shown by willingness to die in the fight. To the soldierly mind, the whole expedition would be ridiculous, causing a feeling of disgust instead of pride. Perhaps a few impudent street-boys might have to have their ears boxed, but otherwise there would be nothing to lend dignity to the expedition.

However, we will suppose the invading army arrived in London, where they would evict the King from Buckingham Palace and the Members from the House of Commons. A few able bureaucrats would be brought over from Berlin to consult with the Civil Servants in Whitehall as to the new laws by which the reign of Kultur was to be inaugurated. No difficulty would be expected in managing so tame a nation, and at first almost all the existing officials would be confirmed in their offices. For the government of a large modern State is a complicated matter, and it would be thought well to facilitate the transition by the help of men familiar with the existing machinery.

But at this point, if the nation showed as much courage as it has always shown in fighting, difficulties would begin. All the existing officials would refuse to co-operate with the Germans. Some of the more prominent would be imprisoned, perhaps even shot, in order to encourage the others. But if the others held firm, if they refused to recognise or transmit any order given by Germans, if they continued to carry out the decrees previously made by the English Parliament and the English Government, the Germans would have to dismiss them all, even to the humblest postman, and call in German talent to fill the breach.

The dismissed officials could not all be imprisoned or shot: since no fighting would have occurred, such wholesale brutality would be out of the question. And it would be very difficult for the Germans suddenly, out of nothing, to create an administrative machine. Whatever edicts they might issue would be quietly ignored by the population. If they ordered that German should be the language taught in schools, the schoolmasters would go on as if no such order had been issued; if the schoolmasters were dismissed, the parents would no longer send the children to school. If they ordered that English young men should undergo military service, the young men would simply refuse; after shooting a few, the Germans would have to give up the attempt in despair. If they tried to raise revenue by customs duties at the ports, they would have to have German customs officers; this would lead to a strike of all the dock labourers, so that this way of raising revenue would become impossible. If they tried to take over the railways, there would be a strike of the railway servants. Whatever they touched would instantly become paralysed, and it would soon be evident, even to them, that nothing was to be made out of England unless the population could be conciliated.

Such a method of dealing with invasion would, of course, require fortitude and discipline. But fortitude and discipline are required in war. For ages past, education has been largely directed to producing these qualities for the sake of war. They now exist so widely that in every civilised country almost every man is willing to die on the battlefield whenever his Government thinks the moment suitable. The same courage and idealism which are now put into war could quite easily be directed by education into the channel of passive resistance. I do not know what losses England may suffer before the present war is ended, but if they amount to a million no one will be surprised. An immensely smaller number of losses, incurred in passive resistance, would prove to any invading army that the task of subjecting England to alien domination was an impossible one. And this proof would be made once for all, without dependence upon the doubtful accidents of war.

In internal politics, in all democratic countries, the very method we have been considering is constantly practised, with continually increasing success. Even in Russia, it was the general strike which secured the Constitution of 1905. For a generation, terrorists had uselessly copied the methods of militarists by bomb-throwing and assassination; they had achieved nothing except to afford the authorities an excuse for ruthless repression—an excuse not only to the public, but also to their own consciences, since they appeared to themselves, as soldiers do, to be brave men facing death in the public service. After all the years of fruitless violence, it was the method of passive non-obedience which secured the momentary victory, afterwards lost through disunion and a return to violence. And in all the dealings of democratic Governments with labour troubles or with irreconcilable minorities, it is this same power of passive resistance that comes into play. In a civilised, highly organised, highly political State, government is impossible without the consent of the governed. Any object for which a considerable body of men are prepared to starve and die can be achieved by political means, without the need of any resort to force. And if this is true of objects only desired by a minority, it is a thousand times more true of objects desired unanimously by the whole nation.

But it may be said that, even if the Germans could not actually take over the government of England, or rob us of internal self-government, they could do two things which would injure us vitally: they could take away our Empire, and they could levy a tribute by the threat of depriving us of food supplies.

The Germans could not take away the self-governing

parts of our Empire, since they would encounter there
the same difficulties as would prevent them from
governing England.   They could take away those
parts of our Empire which we hold by force, and this
would be a blow to our pride: the oppression of subject
races is one of the chief sources of patriotic satisfaction, and one of the chief things for which Germany
envies us.   But it is not a source of pride to any
rational or humane man.   European rule over un-
civilised races is, in fact, a very sordid affair.   The
best of the men whom it employs are those engaged in
the attempt at government, who live in exile and
usually die of fever; the rest grow rich selling rum
to natives or making them work in mines.  Meanwhile
the natives degenerate: some die of drink, some of
diseases caught from white men, some of consumption
in the mines; those who survive contract the vices of
civilisation without losing the vices of barbarism.   It
can only be a blessing to any nation to be deprived of
this source of pride, which is a canker of corruption
and immorality in the life of democratic communities.

That the Germans could levy a tribute on England
by threatening our food supplies is obviously true.
The ethics of such a demand would be exactly the
same as that of the highwayman who demands "your
money or your life."   The same reasons which would
lead a reasonable man to give his money rather than
shoot or be shot would also lead a reasonable nation
to give a tribute rather than resist by force of arms.
The greatest sum that foreigners could theoretically
exact would be the total economic rent of the land and
natural resources of England.   In fact, economic rent

may be defined as what can be, and historically has been, extorted by such means. The rent now paid to landowners in England is the outcome of the exactions made by William the Conquerer and his barons. The law-courts are the outcome of those set up at that time, and the law which they administer, so far as land is concerned, represents simply the power of the sword. From inertia and lack of imagination, the English at the present day continue to pay to the landowners a vast sum to which they have no right but that of conquest. The working classes, the shopkeepers, manufacturers, and merchants, the literary men, and the men of science —all the people who make England of any account in the world—have at most an infinitesimal and accidental share in the rental of England. The men who have a share use their rents in luxury, political corruption, taking the lives of birds, and depopulating and enslaving the rural districts. This way of life is that which almost all English men and women consider the most admirable: those who are anywhere near achieving it struggle to attain it completely, and those who are more remote read serial stories about it as their ancestors would have read of the joys of Paradise.

It is this life of the idle rich which would be curtailed if the Germans exacted a tribute from England. Everything in England that is not positively harmful would be untouched: wages and other earned incomes could not be diminished without diminishing the productivity of English labour, and so lessening England's capacity for paying tribute. Our snobbish instincts, if the idle rich were abolished, might be driven, by want of other outlet, into the admiration of real merit. And if the Germans could effect this for us, they would well deserve their tribute.

It is very doubtful, indeed, whether the Germans would exact from us a larger tribute than we exact from ourselves in resisting them. There is no knowing what this war will have cost England when it ends, but we shall probably not exaggerate if we place the cost at a thousand million pounds.* This represents an annual payment of forty million pounds. All this, together with the annual expenditure on our Army and Navy, we might have paid to the Germans without being any poorer than we shall be when the war ends. This represents an incredibly larger tribute than we derive from India; yet the Germans assure us that we are full of commercial cunning, and that we govern India solely for our own profit. If they believe this, it is hardly to be supposed that the receipt of such a tribute would fail to satisfy them. Meanwhile we should have avoided the death of our young men, the moral degradation of almost our whole population, and the lowering of the standard of civilisation slowly achieved through centuries which were peaceful in comparison with our present condition.

But, of course, all that I have been saying is fantastic, degrading, and out of touch with reality. I have been assuming that men are to some extent guided by reason, that their actions are directed to ends such as "life, liberty, and the pursuit of happiness." This is not the case. Death, slavery, and

---

*It is now (September, 1915) evident that this is an underestimate.

unhappiness (for others) are the chief ends pursued by States in their external relations. It is the preference of such ends to one's own happiness that constitutes patriotism, that shows a man to be free from materialism, and that raises him above the commercial, money-grubbing level of the mere shopkeeper. The Prussian feels himself noble because he is willing to be killed provided men of other nations are killed at the same time. His nobility and his freedom from commercialism consists in the fact that he desires the misery of others more than his own happiness. And there is a Prussian lurking in each of us, ready to make us reject any national advantage which is not purchased by injury to some other nation. It is this lurking Prussian in our instincts who assures us that a policy of non-resistance would be tame and cowardly, unworthy of a great and proud nation, a failure to perform our duty of chastising an exactly similar pride in other nations.

Pride has its place among virtues, in the lives of individuals as well as in the lives of nations. Pride, in so far as it is a virtue, is a determination not to be turned aside from the ends which a man thinks good, no matter what outside pressure may be brought to bear upon him. There is pride in Condorcet, sentenced to the guillotine, spending his last days in writing a book on human progress. There is pride in those who refuse to recant their religious convictions under persecution. Such pride is the noblest form of courage: it shows that self-determination of the will which is the essence of spiritual freedom. But such pride should have as its complement a just conception of what constitutes human welfare, and as it correlative a respect for the freedom of others as absolute as the determination to preserve freedom for ourselves. Exactly the same kind of pride is good in the life of a nation. If we think ill of war, while some other nation thinks well of it, let us show our national pride by living without war, whatever temptations the other nation may put in our way to live according to their ideals rather than according to our own. The Germans, we are given to understand, hate us with a bitter hatred, and long to believe that we feel towards them as they feel towards us; for unrequited hatred is as bitter as unrequited love. They have made it increasingly difficult not to gratify their desire; but in so far as we can keep our resistance free from bitterness we win a spiritual victory over what deserves to be combated in the enemy, which is far more important than any victory to be won by guns and bayonets.

But this kind of pride is not the kind which patriots exhort us to display. The pride that they admire is the kind which aims at thwarting others; it is the pride of power. Having suspected that the Germans desired Morocco and Mesopotamia, we were proud of the fact that we prevented them from acquiring either. Having found that the Boers desired independence, we were proud of the fact that we made them submit to our rule. This kind of pride consists merely in love of dominion. Dominion and power can only be conclusively shown by compelling others to forego what they desire. By a natural consequence, those in whom the love of power is strong are led to inflict pain and to use force against the perfectly legitimate desires of those whom they wish to subdue. In nations, this nation's history are not those who have benefited mankind, but those who have injured other nations. If we prided ourselves upon the good and not the harm that we have done, we should have put Shakespeare in the Nelson Monument, and given Apsley House to Darwin. But the citizens whom every nation honours most are those who have killed the greatest number of foreigners.

It is this pride of power which makes us unwilling to yield to others in matters of no intrinsic importance. The Germans cherish a desire to own African swamps, of which we have a superfluity. No one in England benefits by the possession of them, except a few financial magnates, mostly of foreign origin. If we were reasonable, we should regard the German desire as a curious whim, which we might gratify without any real national loss. Instead of that, we regard the German desire as a crime, and our resistance to it as a virtue. We teach school children to rejoice because so much of the map is painted red. In order that as much as possible may be painted red, we are willing to sacrifice those ideals of freedom which we have led mankind, and, if necessary, to adopt all the worst features of the Prussian spirit. This is because we fear the external enemy, who kills the body, more than the internal enemy, who kills the soul. The soul of a nation, if it is a free soul, without slavishness and without tyranny, cannot be killed by any outward enemy. · And if men would realize this, the panic fear which the nations feel one toward another would be expelled by a better pride than that of diplomatists and war-lords.

The armies and navies of the world are kept up by three causes: cowardice, love of dominion, and lust for blood.

It is cowardice that makes it difficult to meet invasion by the method of passive resistance. More courage and discipline is needed for the successful practice of this method than for facing death in the heat of battle. But I am persuaded that there is in England enough courage and enough capacity for discipline to make success in passive resistance possible, if education and moral teaching is directed to that end instead of to warlike prowess. It is cowardice also that makes men prefer the old method of trying to be stronger than your adversary (in which only one party can succeed), rather than a new method requiring imagination and a readjustment of traditional standards. Yet, if men could think outside the well-worn grooves, there are many plain facts which show the folly of conventional statesmanship. Why has Germany invaded France? Because the French have an army. Why has England attacked Germany? Because the Germans have a navy. Yet people persist in thinking that the French army and the German navy contribute to national safety. Nothing could be more obvious than the facts; nothing could be more universal than men's blindness to them.

The second reason for keeping up the armies and navies of the world is love of dominion. The Germans, in the Morocco controversy, announced that nothing of importance was to happen anywhere without their being consulted. We regarded this as monstrous arrogance; but for two centuries we had advanced the same claim as a matter of course. The matters about which diplomatists raise a pother are usually of only microscopic importance to the welfare of ordinary citizens: they are matters involving national " prestige," that is to say, the power of the State to prevent other States from doing as they wish. This power is sometimes partly based on money, but in the main it rests on armies and navies. If our navy had been smaller, we should not have been able to defeat the German desire for an Atlantic port in Morocco. It would have done us no harm if the Germans had acquired Casablanca, but we enjoyed the thought that our fiat kept them out. The procuring of such pleasures is the second purpose served by armies and navies.

The third purpose of armaments—indeed their primary and original purpose, from which all others are derivative—is to satisfy the lust for blood. Fighting is an instinctive activity of males, both animal and human. Human males, being gregarious, naturally fight in packs. It has been found that the pack tends to be more successful against other packs when fighting within the pack is as far as possible prevented. For this purpose, the law and the police have been instituted. But the shedding of human blood is still considered the most glorious thing a man can do, provided he does it in company with the rest of his pack. War, like marriage, is the legally permitted outlet for a certain instinct. But the instinct which leads to war, unlike the instinct which leads to marriage, so far from being necessary to the human race, is wholly harmful

among civilised men. It is an instinct which easily
becomes atrophied in a settled community: many men
have hardly a trace of it. Unfortunately, as men grow
older, their affections and their powers of thought de-
cay. For this reason, and also because power stimulates the love of power, the men who have most influence in government are usually men whose passions
and impulses are less civilised than those of the average citizen. These men—the great financiers, the
Ministers, and some editors of daily papers—use their
position, their knowledge, and their power of dissem-
inating misinformation, to arouse and stimulate the
latent instinct for bloodshed. When they have succeeded, they say that they are reluctantly forced into
war by the pressure of public opinion. Their activities
are exactly analogous to those of men who distribute
indecent pictures or produce lascivious plays. They
ought to be viewed in the same light; but because of
the notion that a wish to kill foreigners is patriotic
and virtuous, they are honoured as men who have deserved well of their country. They provide an outlet
for the impulse to homicide. To gratify this impulse
is the third and ultimate purpose of armies and navies.

All these three motives for armaments—cowardice,
love of dominion, and lust for blood—are no longer in-
eradicable in civilised human nature. All are diminishing under the influence of modern social organisation. All might be reduced to a degree which could
make them almost inocuous, if early education and
current moral standards were directed to that end.
Passive resistance, if it were adopted deliberately by
the will of a whole nation, with the same measure of

courage and discipline which is now displayed in war, might achieve a far more perfect protection for what is good in national life than armies and navies can ever achieve, without demanding the courage and waste and welter of brutality involved in modern war.

Nevertheless, it is hardly to be expected that progress will come in this way, because the imaginative effort required is too great. It is much more likely that it will come as the reign of law within the State has come, by the establishment of a central government of the world, able and willing to secure obedience by force, because the great majority of men will recognise that obedience is better than the present international anarchy. A central government of this kind will command assent, not as a partisan, but as the representative of the interests of the whole. Very soon, resistance to it would be seen to be hopeless, and wars would cease. Force directed by a neutral authority is not open to the same abuse, or likely to cause the same long-drawn conflicts, as force exercised by quarrelling nations each of which is the judge of its own cause. Although I firmly believe that the adoption of passive instead of active resistance would be good if a nation could be convinced of its goodness, yet it is rather to the ultimate creation of a strong central authority that I should look for the ending of war. But war will only end after a great labour has been performed in altering men's moral ideals, directing them to the good of all mankind, and not only of the separate nations into which men happen to have been born.

# WHY NATIONS LOVE WAR [*]

WHEN the war broke out, many normally pacific people, headed by Mr. H. G. Wells, proclaimed their belief that "this is a war which will end war." Yet they were unintentionally illustrating, by their state of mind, the chief reason for doubting whether this war will end war and the chief obstacle which pacifists will have to overcome if their efforts are ever to be crowned with success. It was obvious that those who proclaimed their belief that there would never be another great war were actually enjoying the present war and that, in spite of a conventional recognition that war is a misfortune, they were happier, more alive, suffering less from what Mr. Graham Wallas calls "balked disposition," than in times of peace. Their belief that this war will end war was obviously not based on reason, but on an unconscious effort to reconcile their present enjoyment with their sincere but not deeply felt belief that war is an evil. My object is to analyse and try to understand this widespread enjoyment of war—a phenomenon, as I think, of the very greatest importance, which, from homage to humanitarian ideals, men in this country have not sufficiently emphasised or allowed for, either in their expectations or in their views as to what has occurred throughout Europe.

In the days of crisis preceding the war every nation in Europe (if one can judge by the newspapers, inter-

*Reprinted from *War and Peace*, November, 1914.

preted in the light of what was occurring in England)
went through a certain instinctive development as
definite as falling in love, though much more complex.
It might have been expected that the populations
which must suffer by war would have urged upon their
Governments the importance of attempting to find a
diplomatic solution.    But in fact what occurred was
exactly the opposite: every Government became increasingly popular as war drew nearer, the advantages
of peace were forgotten or recalled coldly without
conviction, and the desire to have done with negotiations was everywhere loudly expressed by enthusiastic
crowds.  If a diplomatic solution had been found at
the last moment, there would have been almost universal disappointment, and every Government would
have had to face fierce attacks for its weakness in
yielding to the arrogance and unscrupulousness of the
enemy.

This whole collective state of mind illustrated an
instinctive disposition of human nature, stronger, no
doubt, in some nations, such as the Germans, than
in others, but present, to some degree, wherever vigour
and vital energy are to be found.

The basis of the whole state of mind is the instinct
of every gregarious animal to co-operate with members of its own herd and to oppose members of other
herds.  There is in the natural man an instinctive dislike and distrust of men whose ways are different, who
are felt as foreign; and round this instinctive dislike
a whole set of appropriate beliefs tend to congregate—
that the foreigner is wicked, that he has hostile designs, and that his customs are impious.  With the

instinctive dislike and distrust goes an impulse to co-operate, for defence or attack, with those who are recognised as not foreigners. It is this double disposition to co-operation and hostility which forms the motive power in patriotism, though it is perhaps surprising that so primitive a feeling can attach itself to somewhat artificial aggregations such as modern States or even alliances of States.

Round this entirely primitive feeling a number of others are grouped in the civilised man's desire for war. There is first of all the desire for excitement—that is to say, for the exercise, actually or in imagination, of instinctive activities normally kept in check by the restraints of civilised life. Love of excitement is not a primitive impulse: it is a desire for the letting loose of some instinct, no matter what, as a relief from a life unduly full of inhibitions. In modern urban populations this is no doubt one of the most powerful incentives to war; but it could not operate without the other more direct and more primitive impulse as its foundation.

Strong incentives, to many men, are derived from the desires for triumph, for honour, and for power. Under the influence of national self-esteem, every great country believes itself superior to all others in fighting capacity and in courage. Englishmen in times of peace chafe at the thought that their Navy, the greatest in the world, has no opportunity of showing its merits; Germans, similarly, have longed to show the excellence of their Army. Every man believes that the fighting forces of his own country will prove, on the battlefield, to be far better than the enemy has supposed, and will win honour at the expense of the enemy. This is a widespread popular feeling, probably more operative among ordinary citizens than among those who direct policy or have a close knowledge of public affairs. On the other hand the pleasure in the contemplation of the power which victory will bring operates most among those who have an intimate knowledge of modern history or current politics: the pleasure of redrawing (in imagination) the map of Europe has blinded many of the educated classes both here and in Germany to the ravages and inhumanity of war. All these pleasures, which, if they stood alone, would be recognised as somewhat base, are liberated and excused by the fear of what the enemy would do if he were not defeated.

War is felt to be the ultimate test of a nation's manhood, the ultimate proof of its vigour and of its right to exist. In war there can be no doubt that both sides are in earnest; to force one's will on the enemy in so terrific a contest is regarded as unanswerable evidence of superiority in those qualities of courage and determination which most men honour above all others and above all others wish to be known to possess. For this reason the victorious side always tries to persuade itself that its victory has not been due to superior numbers; and for this reason victory with the bayonet gives more pleasure than victory by a more skilful use of artillery.

With this desire to prove the nation's manhood goes the feeling which makes it so difficult to give way in negotiations, the fear of seeming craven or mean-spirited. Even if reason clearly shows the desirability of giving way, even if the point is one which would be readily conceded if not demanded with overt or covert threats, it becomes impossible to give way as soon as fear may be supposed to be the motive. The feeling of shame that would accompany yielding under such circumstances is one of the strongest reasons for the popular clamour in favour of war which arises as soon as a crisis becomes acute.

Besides all these motives there is another, more idealistic, almost religious: a passionate devotion to the Nation, conceived as an entity with a life of its own, surviving the lives of the present citizens, and passing on to their children, the better or the worse for what is done now. With this passionate devotion goes a desire for self-sacrifice, for immolation to further an end greater than anything in any individual life. This impulse of heroism for the welfare of the nation is more widespread than any other kind of subordination to something outside Self, with the sole exception of parental affection. It is by far the noblest of the motives that make for war, and it ought not to be combated by merely material considerations such as the economic exhaustion produced by war.

Being itself in essence religious, like the impulses that lead to martyrdom, it can only be adequately combated by a wider religion, extending the boundaries of one's country to all mankind. But by this extension it loses the support and reinforcement of the primitive gregarious instinct underlying patriotism, and thus becomes, except in a few men gifted with an exceptional power of love, a very pale and thin feeling compared to the devotion that leads a man to face death

willingly on the battlefield. It is this fact, more perhaps than any other, which causes the difficulties of
pacifism.

I do not wish, however, to suggest any pessimism
as to the possibility of leading civilised nations to
abandon the practice of war. The primitive instinct
of collective hostility to strangers, which is at the basis
of popular love of war, depends, like other instincts,
upon its appropriate stimulus. No hostility is more
instinctive than that of cat and dog, yet a cat and a
dog brought up together will become good friends. In
like manner, familiarity with foreigners, absence of
journalistic incitements to fear and suspicion, realisation that their likeness to ourselves is much greater
than their unlikeness, will entirely prevent the growth
of the impulse to go to war. The desires for triumph
and power can be satisfied by the ordinary contests of
football and politics, unless the nation's pride is
embodied in large and efficient armaments. The
feeling that war is the ultimate test of a nation's manhood depends upon a rather barbarous standard of
values, a belief that superiority in physical force is
the most desirable form of superiority. This belief has
largely died out as between individuals in a civilised
country, and it seems not Utopian to hope that it may
die out as between nations. The day may come when
we shall be as proud of Shakespeare as of Nelson.

The same change in a nation's standard of values
will alter the direction of the quasi-religious devotion
to one's native country. If victory in a contest of
material force ceases to be considered the supreme
good for a nation, the desire to be of service will find

other channels than war and will no longer be bound up with injury to other nations. Patriotism in its present form is essentially an ideal involving strife and therefore partial and inadequate; with a better conception of what constitutes a nation's good the element of strife would disappear.

It is important, in any case, to arrive at a true diagnosis of the impulses which lead nations to war. There are times—especially the time immediately after a war—when nations are in a pacific mood and anxious to find ways of preventing future conflicts. It may be hoped that Europe as a whole will be in a pacific mood for some time after the end of the present war; and if the utmost permanent good is to result from the hopes of such a period, it is before all things necessary that the cause of war should be thoroughly understood. I do not believe this is to be found merely in the sins of statesmen, but rather in the standards and desires which civilised nations have inherited from a barbarous past. If this is the case, a stable peace can only be attained by a process of popular education and by a gradual change in the standards of value accepted by men who are considered to be civilised.

# FUTURE OF ANGLO-GERMAN RIVALRY

If the Germans are to be believed, their only implacable and unappeasable enmity in the war is against England.

Toward France they express a kind of brutal, contemptuous liking. As providing opportunities for military glory in 1870 and again last August, France has deserved well of the Fatherland. Toward Russia they have the tolerance of merely momentary hostility, with the consciousness that the grounds of quarrel are finite and capable of adjustment. But toward England they express a hatred which nothing can satisfy except the utter destruction of England's power. Portugal, Spain, Holland, were once great maritime and colonial empires, but they are fallen from their high estate; so England is to fall, if Germany in its present mood is to have its way.

This attitude is not confined to journalists or the thoughtless multitude; it is to be found equally in the deliberate writings of learned men. Very instructive from this point of view is an article by the historian Eduard Meyer, in the Italian periodical *Scientia*, on England's war against Germany and the problems of the future.* The erudite professor, following Mommsen, considers Germany as the analogue of Rome and England as the analogue of Carthage. He hardly hopes for a decisive victory now, but looks

*Reprinted from the *Atlantic Monthly*, July, 1915.
*"Englands Krieg gegen Deutschland und die Probleme der Zukunft"; March, 1915, pp. 286-300.

forward to a succession of conflicts like the Punic
Wars, ending, we are to suppose, in an equally final
triumph. "Especially in America," he says, "but
also in Europe, above all in the neutral countries,
there are not a few well-meaning people who believe
that this tremendous war will be the last for a long
time to come, that a new era of peaceful development
and of harmonious international peace will follow.  I
regard these views as a Utopian dream.  Their realisation could be hoped for only in case we should
succeed in really casting England to the ground,
breaking her maritime dominion, and thereby conquering the freedom of the seas, and at the same time
in so controlling our other enemies that they would
lose for ever the desire to attack us again.  But so
high our hopes can hardly rise; it seems far more
probable that we shall have to be content with much
less, even if we remain victorious to the end.  But
then, so far as one can foresee, this peace will only
be a short truce; England will use the first opportunity of beginning the fight again, better prepared,
at the head of a new coalition if not of the old one,
and a long series of difficult and bloody wars will
follow, until at last the definite decision is obtained."
He adds that modern civilisation, from now on, is to
decline, as ancient civilisation declined; that the era
of attempts at international friendship is definitely
past, and that "the characteristic of the next century
will be unconquerable opposition and embittered hate
between England and Germany."

Very similar sentiments are expressed by English
professors, except that their military hopes are less

modest, and they expect to achieve in this war that crushing victory which, like Eduard Meyer, they regard as the only possible road to a permanent peace. They hope, at any rate, to crush German militarism, and Professor Meyer assures us that "whoever intends to destroy German militarism must destroy the German nation."*

Are the professors of England and Germany in the right? Is it certain that these two nations will continue to fight and hate each other until one of them is utterly broken? Fortunately, no country consists wholly of professors, not even Germany; and it may be hoped that more sanity is to be found among those who have not been made mad by much learning. For the moment, both countries are wholly blind to their own faults, and utterly fantastic in the crimes which they attribute to the enemy. A vast but shadowy economic conflict has been invented to rationalise their hostility, which in fact is as irrational and instinctive as that of dogs who snarl and fly at each other in the street. The cynic who said, "Speech has been given us to conceal our thoughts," might well have added, "Thought has been given us to conceal our passions from ourselves." At least I am sure that this is true of thought in war-time.

In this article, I wish to examine, in a neutral spirit, the causes and supposed justifications of Anglo-German enmity, and to suggest ways by which it may be possible hereafter to avoid the appalling consequences contemplated by Professor Meyer.

---

*English professors now (September, 1915) have come into almost exact agreement with Eduard Meyer.

The first thing that must strike any impartial observer of England and Germany in war-time is their amazing similarity in myth and melodrama. France and Russia each has its myth, for without myth no great national upheaval is possible. But their myths are different from ours, whereas the myths of England and Germany are all but identical. Each believes itself a great peace-loving nation, powerful, but always using its power to further worthy ends. Each believes that the other, with an incredible perfidy inspired by the basest jealousy, suddenly stirred up the war, after many years of careful preparation, military in the one case, diplomatic in the other. Each believes that only the utter humiliation of the other can secure the peace of the world and the ordered progress of civilisation. In each, a pacifist minority urges moderation in the use of victory, while yielding to none in the conviction that victory is the indispensable preliminary to any future reconstruction. Each is absolutely confident of victory, and prepared for any sacrifice, however great, in order to secure victory. Each is quite unable to believe that the other is sincere in the opinion which it professes: its own innocence and the other's guilt are as clear as noonday, and can be denied only by the most abject hypocrisy.

Both cannot be right in these opinions, and *a priori* it is not likely that either is right. No nation was ever so virtuous as each believes itself, and none was ever so wicked as each believes the other. If these beliefs survive the war, no real peace will be possible. Both nations have concentrated their energies so

wholly on making war that they have rendered it
almost impossible to make peace. In normal times
civilised and humane people find a difficulty in be-
lieving that they do well to butcher each other. In
order to overcome this feeling, journalists have filled
the minds of their readers with such appalling
accounts of the enemy's crimes that hatred has come
to seem a noble indignation, and it has grown difficult
to believe that any of our opponents deserve to live.
Yet peace, if it is to be real, must be accompanied by
respect, and must bring with it some sense of justice
toward rival claims. What these claims are, and what
justice demands if they are to be reconciled, must be
realised in some degree before the peace, if the peace
is to heal the wounds which the war is inflicting.

Apart from accusations of crime connected with the
war, what have been the grounds of England's opposition to Germany in recent years?

Far the most important ground has been fear of the
German navy, not as it has hitherto been, but as it
may become. It is said on the Continent—not only
by Germans—that jealousy of Germany's economic
development was an equal cause of hostility; but I
believe this to be an entire mistake. America's economic development has been quite as remarkable as
that of Germany, but it has not produced the slightest
ripple of political hostility. The government in
power, as free traders,* do not believe that the prosperity of one country is economically injurious to that
of another, and in this opinion a majority of the

---

*This was written before the Coalition Government was
formed.

nation agree with them. Most Germans think of trade in nationalist terms, but in England this habit is not very common. And whatever may be thought abroad, it is contrary to British political instincts to allow trade rivalry to cause diplomatic opposition—largely, no doubt, because we realise that a nation's trade is not necessarily injured by defeat in war.

But whoever threatens our naval supremacy touches a sensitive nerve, awakening an instinctive movement of self-protection in all classes, even the most uneducated and the least conscious of international complications. When the Germans, with their usual incautious explicitness, made the announcement, "Our future is on the sea," most Englishmen felt, almost without conscious thought, that the Germans might as well have announced that their future lay through the death of England's greatness and the starvation of our population. In vain the Germans protested that their navy was purely defensive, and was not intended to be as strong as ours. As we watched the carrying out of their Navy Law, as we realised how the era of dreadnoughts had diminished our superiority, something not far removed from apprehension began to be felt; and in a proud nation apprehension inevitably shows itself in hostility. Because the apprehension was real and deep-seated, the hostility was rather blind and instinctive; although, in the region of conscious thought, the hopes of an understanding were not abandoned, yet in that deeper region out of which effective action springs, the belief in a future conflict had taken root and could no longer be dislodged.

At the same time Germany's growing friendship

with Turkey produced uneasiness in our governing classes, with whom the consciousness of Indian problems has become almost as much part of the texture of everyday thought as the need of naval supremacy. Our traditional policy of protecting the Turk, while it had caused untold misery in the Balkans, had been maintained chiefly on account of the Mohammedan population of India. When the Kaiser supplanted us at Constantinople, and announced himself the protector of all Mohammedans, we dreaded the effect on the most warlike races of India; and our dread was not diminished by the Bagdad Railway, with the prospect which it opened of German colonisation in Mesopotamia and a German naval base on the Persian Gulf. But this motive, although it affected our government and that small section of the population which is alive to Indian problems, did not, like the challenge to our sea-power, affect all classes or attain the status of a question to be discussed at general elections. Moreover, this whole problem was in its nature capable of diplomatic adjustment by mutual concessions; indeed, we are told that an agreement had almost been concluded when the war broke out.

Let us now try to see the history of the past fifteen years from the German point of view. Before speaking of their supposed grievances, I wish to say that I regard the whole theory out of which they spring as wholly mistaken: I do not believe that it is of any real importance to a nation to possess colonies or to develop either its military or its naval forces beyond the point which is necessary to prevent invasion. This, however, is not the official English view; and the official

German view seems, apart from questions of method, merely an echo of the principles by which English policy has been governed for centuries. It is only this similarity—not absolute validity—that I wish to exhibit in stating the German case.

The Germans are commonly regarded as an exceptionally aggressive nation. This is no doubt true of their spirit, but when we come to inquire into their actual acquisitions, we find that in recent years their gains of territory have been insignificant in comparison with those of England and Russia, and approximately equal to those of France. Since 1900, we have gained the Transvaal and the Orange Free State, we have consolidated our position in Egypt, and we have secured a protectorate over Southern Persia and its oil wells. The French, meanwhile, have gained about four-fifths of Morocco, and the Russians, though they have lost a small portion of Manchuria, have gained more than half of Persia. The Germans, in the same period, have gained only a not very valuable colony in West Africa.* Their designs in Morocco and Mesopotamia have been thwarted, largely by England's efforts. Yet they feel that their economic

*The following figures are not without interest:—

Total area of colonies.

| | |
|---|---|
| Great Britain | 11,429,078 square miles |
| France | 4,512,543 " " |
| Germany | 1,027,820 " " |

Increase in area of colonies since 1900.

| | |
|---|---|
| Great Britain | 324,500 square miles |
| Germany | 100,820 " " |
| France | 92,180 " " |

The British increase consists almost wholly of the Transvaal, tion of the Congo ceded to Germany in 1911; and the German French increase consists almost wholly of Morocco, less the por- the Orange Free State, and the British sphere in Persia. The increase consists wholly of this portion of the Congo, less a small area in the Cameroons, ceded to France in 1911. The Russian sphere in Persia contains 305,000 square miles and 6,400,000 inhabitants.

progress and their growing population make the need of colonies far greater for them than for the French.

I am not for a moment denying that we had weighty reasons for our opposition to German expansion, though perhaps weightier reasons could have been found for not opposing it. I am only concerned, for the moment, with the way in which our actions impressed the Germans, not with the justification of our actions. The Germans, in spite of their progress, their energy, and their population, are very inferior in colonial possessions, not only to England and Russia, but also to France. This seems to them unjust; but wherever they turn to try to acquire new colonies, England and England's navy block the way, because of our friendship with France, or our sensitiveness about India, or some other interest in the complicated web of our foreign policy.

German aggressiveness, real and obnoxious as it has become, is the result of experience. Germany cannot, as we do, acquire colonies absent-mindedly, without intention, and almost without effort. When colonies were easier to acquire than they are now, Germany had not yet entered into the competition; and since Germany became a great Power, it has been handicapped by naval inferiority and by the necessity of defending two frontiers. It is these accidents of history and geography, rather than innate wickedness, which have produced German aggressiveness. The aims of German policy are closely similar to those which we have always pursued, but its methods cannot be the unobtrusive methods which we have usually adopted, because such methods, in the circumstances, would achieve nothing.

Colonial ambitions are no doubt one reason why Germany has developed a navy; but another and still more imperative reason is the necessity of safeguarding foreign trade.

In the time of Bismarck, Germany had not yet become a great industrial nation: it was independent of foreign food, and its exports of manufactures were insignificant. Its industrial expansion dates from the introduction of the Bessemer process in 1879, by which its supplies of iron became possible to work at a profit. From that time onward, German industrial progress has been extraordinarily rapid; more and more, Germany has tended to become dependent, like England, upon the possibility of importing food and exporting manufactures. In this war, as we see, Germany is just able, by very painful economy, to subsist upon the stock of food in the country; but another ten years of such development as was taking place before the war would have made this impossible. High agrarian protection, which alone could have retarded the process, was naturally disliked by the manufacturers and the working classes, and could not be carried beyond a certain point for fear of leading to a triumph of Socialism.

It thus became obvious that, in a few years' time, Germany would be liable to defeat by starvation in any war with a superior naval power. In 1900, when the Germans decided to build a great navy, the Triple Alliance was weaker than France and Russia on the sea. The wish not to be inferior to France and Russia is enough to account for the beginnings of the German navy; the rivalry with us may perhaps have been no part of the original intention, but merely a result of the suspicions produced in England by the German programme. However that may be, it ought to have been obvious to the Germans that a strong navy was sure to make us hostile, and would therefore not serve the purposes for which it was intended unless it was stronger than our navy. But it could not be supposed that we should submit to the existence of a navy stronger than our own, unless we had first been utterly and hopelessly defeated; and there was no way of defeating us except by first having a navy stronger than ours. For these reasons, the German policy was inherently incapable of success. And yet, without success, all industrial progress and all colonial expansion remain perpetually at England's mercy. If we ask ourselves how we should feel if we were similarly at the mercy of Germany, we shall perhaps begin to understand why the Germans hate us. And yet we can hardly feel any sense of guilt, because a supreme navy is for us a matter of life and death.

This dilemma must be faced, if we are to understand the conflict of England and Germany, and not regard it as merely due to wickedness on one side or on the other. After the war, sooner or later, exactly the same problem will have to be faced again. The native energy of the Germans cannot be permanently checked by defeat: after a longer or shorter period of recuperation, they will again feel that commercial safety and colonial expansion demand a strong navy, if they are not to be content to live on sufferance and to be com-

pelled to bow to England's will on all occasions of
serious dispute. The problem is a new one, since
hitherto England has been the only nation dependent
for subsistence on food imported by sea, and England
has had unquestioned naval supremacy. But if we
are to avoid the century of internecine warfare contemplated by Eduard Meyer, we must find some solution of the problem, and not be content merely to
hope that, whenever war comes, we shall be victorious.
Germany's industrial ambitions, at least, are entirely
legitimate; and they alone make some security for
German trade an imperative necessity. It is not only
justice that makes it necessary to find a solution, but
also self-preservation. It is impossible to know how
submarines may develop; perhaps, in future, no
degree of naval power will be sufficient to protect sea-
borne trade. Even now, our position might be preca-
rious if all the men and money which Germany has
devoted to useless dreadnoughts had been devoted to
the multiplication of submarines. After the war, our
own future safety, as well as the peace of the world,
will demand some new and statesmanlike development
in our naval policy.

No solution will be possible until it grows clear to
the Germans that they cannot reasonably hope to
become superior to us at sea. So long as that hope
remains with them, they will go on struggling to
acquire that complete world-dominion which they
believe would result from possession of both the
strongest navy and the strongest army in the world.
It is to be expected that the present war will persuade
them of the futility of their hopes. They speak to

neutrals of their wish to secure for all nations "the freedom of the sea," but the neutrals remain deaf to all their blandishments. The neutrals do not see how there would be more freedom under German supremacy than under that of England, and they do see that, so long as any nation has naval supremacy, it is better that it should be a nation without a strong army or the means of invasion. This will enable us to avoid hostile coalitions, and to make a German victory over us at some future date exceedingly unlikely. But it will not, by itself, prevent Germany from hating us, or from seeking every possible means of injuring us. And if Germany's industrial development continues, it will leave Germany increasingly dependent upon us for its means of subsistence in any war in which Russia is on our side.

Such a situation will be full of danger to the peace of Europe and of possible harm to ourselves as well as to Germany. For the sake of the progress of civilisation, and also for the sake of our security as well as Germany's, both nations, if they have any statesmanship, will be driven to seek some means by which food-supply can be secured from the menace of attack by a hostile Power.

Before this war, many would have thought that abolition of the right of capture at sea would achieve this object. But it is now evident that no reliance can be placed upon paper guarantees which are not backed by force. If it could be expected that a nation which resorted to capture at sea would have to face a coalition of neutrals, the practice of capture might be effectively abolished. But so long as neutrals do not intervene by force of arms to protect international law, it cannot be expected that its provisions will be observed; nor would they be observed if neutrals should intervene, unless they were sufficiently powerful to turn the scale. If Germany's submarine blockade could have been made effective, all the neutrals in the world would have been powerless to prevent it.

In this matter, as also in regard to armies, the future of civilisation depends on the discovery of means which will make nations strong for defence but weak for attack. The naval problem is particularly urgent, because, if submarines develop as may be expected, navies will become strong for attack and weak for defence, "attack" being understood as including the capture or destruction of merchant ships.

There is one obvious solution, which would be adopted if any large section of mankind were actuated by humanity or reason or even self-interest. If this were the case, national armies and navies would be abolished, and only an international army and navy would be retained, for police purposes. But among all the great Powers, pride is stronger than self-interest; men prefer the risk of death for themselves and their sons, the certainty of impoverishment and the possibility of national disaster, to loss of the opportunity for bullying which is afforded by an army and a navy. Under these circumstances, there is probably no chance of a theoretically complete solution of the problem. The best hope is that through the experience of the present war men will acquire a more firm resolve to preserve the peace, and neutrals will realise that war is a disaster even to those who do not take part in it. It may be that, in time, the powers not directly interested in a quarrel will insist upon its being always submitted to an international tribunal, and will make their insistence effective by threatening war if it is disregarded. In that case, any Power could secure safety by merely abstaining from aggression. At present, no great Power wishes to make aggression impossible. But experience of war, the progress of democracy, and the growing economic interdependence of different countries, are causing rapid changes in public opinion. It is at least as rational to expect that the next hundred years will see the growth and victory of an international council for the settlement of all disputes between nations, as it is to expect, with Eduard Meyer, that they will see civilisation engulfed in a futile contest for supremacy between England and Germany.

The learned historian, I am confident, does injustice to his compatriots; I know that he does injustice to the English. Without hope, nothing will be achieved; but with hope, no limits can be set to what may be achieved toward realising the ideal of international co-operation. Is the victory of either side in this war likely to bring a stable peace? Both in England and in Germany, men who have professed a horror of war, but who do not wish it thought that they oppose this war, have argued that their own country is notorious for its love of peace, of which it has given repeated proofs, laying it open to the charge of weakness; but that it has been attacked by unscrupulous enemies, and must quell their ruthless pride before the world can be relieved from the dread of war. This language is not insincere, but is the result of a very superficial analysis of the events and passions which led up to the conflict. Such an analysis, if allowed to pass unchallenged, is dangerous, since it leaves untouched all the misjudgment, suspicion, and pride out of which future wars, equally devastating, may be expected to grow in the course of the years. Something more than the mere victory of one party is necessary for a secure peace, and something deeper than a belief in the enemy's wickedness is necessary if the nations are to move towards that goal. I shall attempt first an analysis of the causes of modern war, and then a discussion of means of preventing future wars between civilised States.

# IS A PERMANENT PEACE POSSIBLE?*

## I.

. The present war springs from the rivalry of States.
And the rivalry of States springs from certain erron-
eous beliefs, inspired and encouraged by pride and
fear, and embodied in a political machinery intended
to make the power of a State quick, effective, and
terrible. If wars between civilised States are to
cease, these beliefs must be seen to be mistaken, pride
must take a different form, fear must become groundless, and the machinery of international relations must
no longer be designed solely for rivalry.

In surveying the larger causes of the war, the
diplomacy of the last fortnight may be left altogether
out of account. Ever since the conclusion of the
Anglo-French *entente* in 1904 the war had been on
the point of breaking out, and could only have been
avoided by some radical change in the temper of
nations and Governments. The annexation of Alsace-
Lorraine had produced a profound estrangement between France and Germany. Russia and Germany
became enemies through the Pan-Slavist agitation,
which threatened the Austrian influence in the Balkans and even the very existence of the Austro-Hun-
garian State. Finally the German determination to
build a powerful Navy drove England into the arms
of Russia and France. Our long-standing differences
with those two countries were suddenly discovered

---

*Reprinted from the *Atlantic Monthly*, March, 1915.

to be unimportant, and were amicably arranged without any difficulty. By a treaty whose important articles were kept secret, the French withdrew their opposition to our occupation of Egypt, and we undertook to support them in acquiring Morocco—a bargain which, from our own point of view, had the advantage of reviving the hostility between France and Germany at a time when there seemed a chance of its passing away. As regards Russia, our deep-rooted suspicions of its Asiatic designs were declared groundless, and we agreed to the independence of Tibet and the partition of Persia in return for an acknowledgment of our suzerainty in Afghanistan. Both these arrangements show that, if good will and reason presided over international affairs, an adjustment of differences might have been made at any time; as it is, nothing but fear of Germany sufficed to persuade us of the uselessness of our previous hostility to France and Russia.

No sooner had this grouping of the European Powers been brought about than the *Entente* and the Alliance began a diplomatic game of watchful manoeuvring against each other. Russia suffered a blow to her pride in the Austrian annexation of Bosnia and Herzegovina; Germany felt humiliated by having to acknowledge, though with compensation, the French occupation of Morocco. The first Balkan war was a gain to Russia, the second afforded some consolation to Austria. And so the game went on, with recurring crises and alternate diplomatic victories first for one side, then for the other.

In all this struggle, no one on either side thought

for a moment of the welfare of the smaller nations which were the pawns in the struggle. The fact that Morocco appealed to Germany for protection against French aggression was not held to put England and France in the wrong. The fact that the Persians— the intellectual aristocracy of the Moslem world—had freed themselves from the corrupt Government of the Shah and were becoming Liberal and Parliamentary was not regarded as any reason why their northern provinces should not be devastated by Cossacks and their southern regions occupied by the British. The fact that the Turks had for ages displayed a supremacy in cruelty and barbarism by torturing and degrading the Christians under their rule was no reason why Germany should not, like England in former times, support their tottering despotism by military and financial assistance. All considerations of humanity and liberty were subordinated to the great game: first one side threatened war, then the other; at last both threatened at once, and the patient populations, incited cynically by lies and clap-trap, were driven on to the blind work of butchery.

A world where such cruel absurdities are possible is not to be put right by a mere treaty of peace. War between civilised States is both wicked and foolish, and it will not cease until either the wickedness or the folly is understood by those who direct the policy of nations. Most men do not mind being wicked, and the few who do have learnt ways of persuading themselves that they are virtuous. But, except in moments of passion, men do mind being foolish. There is more hope of preventing war in future by persuading men

of its folly than by urging its wickedness. To a
dispassionate observation its folly is evident, but most
observation is not dispassionate: unconsciously men
tend to adopt the opinions which will justify them in
indulging their passions.  Just as a libertine, in order
to excuse himself, comes to think that women have
no deep feelings, so a militant patriot comes to think
that the interests of his country are vitally opposed
to those of some other country, in order that he may
have an opportunity to indulge pride, the desire for
triumph, and the lust of dominion.  What the pacifist
has to contend against is a system of false beliefs,
inspired by unrecognised evil passions which are
thought to be justified by the beliefs.  If the beliefs
are seen to be false, there is some hope that the
passions may be recognised as evil.  And the falsehood
of the belief in the essential conflict of interests between nations is easily recognised by any candid mind.

Among men, as among all gregarious animals, there
are two kinds of economic relation: co-operation and
competition.  There is co-operation when the activities
which the one undertakes in his own interests tend
to benefit the other; there is competition when they
tend to injure the other.  Neither co-operation nor
competition need be conscious; it is not even necessary
that either should be aware of the existence of the
other.  But in so far as they are conscious they bring
into play quite different sets of feelings.  On the one
side we have affection, loyalty, gratitude; on the other
fear, hatred, triumph.  The emotions out of which war
springs result from a combination of the two sets: they
are the emotions appropriate to co-operation against

a common competitor. In the modern world, where men are grouped by States, these emotions are summed up in patriotism. Co-operation and competition have governed the lives of our ancestors since the days before they were human, and in the course of the struggle for existence our emotional nature has developed so as to respond deeply and instinctively to these ancient stimuli. There is in all men a disposition to seek out occasions for the exercise of instinctive feelings, and it is this disposition, rather than any inexorable economic or physical fact, which is at the bottom of enmities between nations. The conflicts of interest are invented to afford an excuse for feelings of hostility; but as the invention is unconscious, it is supposed that the hostility is caused by some real conflict of interests.

The cause of this absence of harmony between our instincts and our real needs is the modern development of industry and commerce. In a savage community, where each family lives by its own labour, there is no occasion for *peaceful* co-operation in any group larger than the family. But there is often occasion for *war-like* co-operation: if all the members of some other tribe can be killed, it is possible to appropriate their hunting grounds and their pastures. In such a state of things, war is profitable to the victors, and the vanquished leave no descendants. The human race is descended from a long line of victors in war; for, although there have been just as many vanquished, they failed in early days to leave any posterity. The feelings which men now have on the subject of war and international relations are feelings

which were in agreement with facts, so far as the
victors were concerned, in those primitive internecine
combats of savage tribes.  But in the modern world
our economic organisation is more civilised than our
emotions, and the conflicts in which we indulge do not
really offer that prospect of gain which lets loose
the brute within us.  The brute within us refuses to
face this disappointing fact, and turns upon those
who bring it forward with savage accusations of un-
manliness or lack of patriotism.  But it remains a
fact none the less.

The international character of our economic organisation is due to division of labour, taking partly the
form of exchange, partly the form of multiplying
stages in production.  Consider some quite simple
example : say a loaf of bread baked in Holland from
Argentine wheat grown by the help of English agri-
cultural machinery made from Spanish ore.  Holland,
Argentina, England, and Spain all, through this loaf
of bread, have an interest in each other's welfare;
any misfortune to any one of the four is likely to
cause some injury to the other three.  And so it happens that times of good trade and times of bad trade
are both world-wide.  Yet in spite of the fact that when
Germany is prosperous England is prosperous, and
when Germany has hard times England has hard
times, men persist, both in England and in Germany,
in concentrating attention on the comparatively small
amount of economic competition, to the exclusion of
the very much greater amount of economic co-operation.  It is thought that if Germany were ruined
England would be enriched, and *vice versa*.    Yet

every tradesman knows that the ruin of his customers is an injury to him, which cannot be compensated by the ruin of his competitors. Instinct makes us want a nation to hate, and diplomatists have decided that, for the last ten years, that nation should be Germany; and since we hate Germany, we imagine its interests opposed to ours. But one moment's thought without hatred shows that the whole opposition is merely imaginary.

The diplomatic conflict is even more unreal and disproportionate to any possibility of gain than the economic conflict. Apart from the satisfaction of a somewhat childish pride, what does it matter to either France or Germany which of them owns Morocco? Neglecting the fact that France had to promise the open door in order to win Germany's acquiescence, the extreme limit of possible advantage would be the capture of the whole foreign trade of Morocco. This is a limit which cannot, in practice, be reached, since, even with the most restrictive tariff, there will be some commodities which will have to be imported from elsewhere. But even if it could be reached, it is a mere fallacy to suppose that the necessary restrictions would be advantageous to France. England, after much experience, has abandoned the attempt to impose any restrictions on foreign trade in its Crown Colonies, because they hamper the development of colonies, diminish their purchasing power, and in the long run injure English trade more than they benefit it. With every desire to profit by injury to others, experience has taught us that our own profit is best secured by allowing equal opportunities to other nations, and that

injury to others, however delightful in itself, has to be
paid for by a corresponding injury to ourselves. But
even if we adopt, for the sake of argument, the view
that a nation owning a colony can profit by securing
the whole trade of that colony to itself, what proportion is there between the gain and the cost?

In order that the French might acquire Morocco,
England and France, in 1905 and again in 1911, were
brought to the verge of war with Germany, causing
huge increases in the French Army and the English
Navy, embittering the relations of both with Germany,
and producing a state of public feeling which made
the present war possible. A solemn international conference deliberated at Algeciras, and arrived at decisions which England and France regarded as "scraps
of paper." Finally Germany, as the price of abandoning its claims, acquired a bit of African territory,
at the expense of a similar increase of armaments, a
similar exacerbation of public feeling, and an exhibi-
tion of bullying methods which prepared the whole
world to view all Germany's proceedings with suspicion. And as everybody knows, the loss due to mere
uncertainty, produced in industry and finance by a
"Vigorous" policy, was so great that the German
business world at last compelled the Government to
give way. And all this turmoil was on the question
whether France should have the empty right to call
Morocco "French"!

Viewed as a means of obtaining any tangible gain,
a diplomatic contest such as that which was waged
over Morocco is a childish absurdity. The diplomatists who conduct it, and the journalists who

applaud their ridiculous activities, are ignorant men
—ignorant, I mean, in all that is really important to
the welfare of nations. Their only training is in the
kind of skill by which a horse-dealer palms off a bad
bargain upon a foolish customer, and in the knowledge
of personalities which is required in all games of
intrigue. But such training, though it had its importance in simpler times, grows less and less useful as
the organisation of society becomes more complex and
as the interdependence of men in widely severed parts
of the world increases. More and more the important
facts are dry, statistical, impersonal; less and less are
they of the sort that lends itself to expression in
traditional literary form. Men's imaginations are
governed to an extraordinary extent by literary tradition: the fact that the really important knowledge can
only be acquired by industrious investigation makes it
"vulgar" and not such as any aristocratic diplomatist would condescend to know.

The economic absurdity of our diplomatic and
military conflicts is not denied by well-informed advocates of international strife. They will admit that,
in a war between civilised States, even the victor
can no longer hope to gain in wealth. But they reply
that such considerations are sordid, and that they, the
war-like party, have nobler ideals than mere money-
grubbing. This is an even more preposterous absurdity than the pretence of trading advantages to be
obtained by victory. Let us admit at once that the
interest which most people felt in the Moroccan question was not, except in a very small degree, an

economic interest. But was it something higher than an economic interest?

The main thing involved in all such contests, and the thing that makes the average man tolerate them, is national pride. The Germans felt that France had failed to treat them with proper respect by not informing them officially of the Anglo-French agreement; the English and French felt the sending of the Panther to Agadir an act of aggression which must be resented; the Germans felt Mr. Lloyd George's high language at the Mansion House in 1911 a threat to which no great Power could yield with dignity. This is the nobler stuff with which the idealists of war confront the money-grubbing economists! Compared with this schoolboy desire for cheap triumphs, money-grubbing is humane, enlightened, and noble. The man who builds up an industry confers benefits upon countless others in the course of pursuing his own advantage: he becomes rich because he is doing something of real use to the community. But the pride that wishes to humiliate, and the pride that *can* be humiliated by yielding trivial diplomatic advantages rather than risk war, are alike childish and barbarous, springing from low ambitions, and enviously regarding one man's gain as consisting in another's loss. Diplomatic victory rests with the side most willing to risk war: so long as men feel proud of their country on account of its victories, and not on account of its contributions to civilisaton and the welfare of mankind, so long they will feel humiliated when their country is reasonable, and elated when it is brutal, overbearing, ready to plunge the world into the chaos of armed conflict. As against this state of mind, the man who urges the economic loss involved, nowadays, even in successful war, is a humane advocate of sane co-operation, not a man blinded by sordid considerations to the supposed splendours of what is really the most degraded form of "patriotism."

The disease from which the civilised world is suffering is a complex one, derived from the failure of men's instincts to keep pace with changing material conditions. Among savages, where there is no trade and little division of labour, the only economic relation between different tribes is that of competition for the food supply. The tribe which attacks with most cunning and ferocity exterminates the greatest number of others, and leaves the largest posterity. Disposition to ferocity and cunning is, at this stage, a biological advantage; and the instincts of civilised men are those developed during this early stage. But through the growth of commerce and manufactures it has come about that nine-tenths of the interests of one civilised nation coincide with nine-tenths of the interests of any other. So long as the disposition to primitive ferocity is not excited, men are able to see their community of interest, as, for example, most men do in America. But there remains in the background a readiness to enmity and suspicion, a capacity for all the emotions of the savage on the war-path, which can be roused by any skillful manipulator; and there remain many men who, from a brutal nature or from some underground effect of self-interest, are unable to see that friendship between nations is possible and that hostility has lost whatever *raison d'être* it once possessed. And so the old rivalries, now become an unmeaning and murderous futility, go on unchecked, and all the splendid heroism of war is wasted on a tragic absurdity.

## II.

The old methods have brought us to the present disaster, and new and better methods must be found. So much is agreed on all hands.

But as soon as we attempt to specify better methods, disagreement breaks out—partly from disagreement as to the facts which have brought about the present situation, partly from desire to find an heroic solution which shall once for all make war impossible by some mechanical arrangement.

The steps to be taken for securing a lasting peace fall into three parts: (1) the conditions of peace; (2) the subsequent machinery for adjusting international disputes; (3) measures for producing, throughout Europe, a more sane, well-informed, and pacific public opinion.

(1) Nine men out of ten, in the combatant nations, consider, or at least considered when the war broke out, that the conditions of peace are the only question of importance. Nine out of ten Englishmen believe, or believed, that England, France, and Russia are essentially peace-loving countries; that they made every conceivable effort for the preservation of peace; and that the one thing necessary to secure the permanent peace of the world is that they should smash the military power of Germany and Austria. Nine out of ten Germans believe, or believed, that Germany and Austria are essentially peace-loving countries; that

while they were struggling to preserve the peace, Russia, secretly encouraged by England treacherously mobilised under cover of negotiations between the Tsar and the Kaiser; and that the one thing necessary to secure the permanent peace of the world is that Germany and Austria should smash the military power of the Allies. These opposing views are merely melodramatic: no nation is quite black, and none is quite white, but all are of varying shades of grey. Like every one else in Europe, I think my own nation of the lightest shade of grey; but no member of the game of Alliance and Entente, which statesmen have played for the last ten years, ought to flatter itself that it is wholly unspotted. And in any case, as a solution, the complete destruction of the enemy has the defect of being impossible. England and Germany will both exist after the war: if they fought each other for five centuries, like England and France, they would still both exist. This fact is beginning to be realised on both sides, and to compel even the most bellicose to seek for some way by which they can learn to endure each other's existence with equanimity. What is wanted is a change of heart, leading to a change of political methods; and victory or defeat must be considered in the light of their power of producing a change of heart.

From this point of view, it is important that no nation should make such great gains as to feel that it was worth while going to war, and that none should suffer such humiliating losses as to be impelled to revenge. The result of 1870 was the worst possible from the point of view of mankind. The Germans were encouraged in militarism by success, the French were goaded into militarism by the intolerable shame of defeat and dismemberment. Whatever happens at the peace, there should be no new Alsace-Lorraines: any transfer of territory should be such as can be recommended to neutral opinion on the ground of the wishes of the inhabitants. So far as the West is concerned, it may be reasonably hoped that this condition will be carried out; but in the East it is to be feared that none of the combatants will respect it. No one supposes that any part of the Turkish Empire will be allowed any voice in deciding its fate; but it must be admitted that the Turks, throughout all the centuries since their rise, have done as little to deserve consideration as any nation on earth.

(2) But changes of territory are the least important part of what may be hoped from the peace. In all nations, every sane man and woman will desire a completely new system in international affairs. The only men who will desire to prolong the present system are statesmen, sensational journalists, and armament makers—the men who profit by slaughter, either in credit or in cash, without running any risk of being slaughtered themselves. Since these men will control the actual Congress, they will be able to postpone the inauguration of a happier age, unless America undertakes the championship of mankind against the warring governments. All humane people in Europe would wish America to participate: if possible, they would wish the Congress to take place in the neutral atmosphere of Washington, with Mr. Wilson as its President. The Governments may oppose this plan,

from the wish of officials to retain power in their own hands, and of combatants to avoid having to hear the voice of reason. But public opinion is against the Governments in this question, though for the moment it has difficulty in expressing itself.

New methods in international affairs are required not in the interests of one side or the other, but in the interests of mankind, lest civilisation and humanity should perish from the world. It would be disastrous if new methods were imposed by the victors upon the vanquished as part of the humiliation of defeat: they ought to be adopted by all, at the suggestion of neutrals, as an escape from the tragic entanglement which has dragged a horrified Europe, as though by the compulsion of an external Fate, into a cataclysm not desired beforehand by one man in a hundred in any of the nations involved in the struggle. In every nation, men believe they are fighting for the defence of home and country against wanton aggression, bcause they know that they themselves have not desired war, and they know or suspect the sins of foreign governments while they are ignorant of the sins of their own. In every nation when this war comes to an end, men will welcome any means of avoiding the risk of another such war in the future.

Most of the friends of peace are agreed in advocating some kind of International Council to take cognisance of all disputes between nations and to urge what it regards as a just solution. But it is not easy to agree either as to the powers or as to the composition of Council.

The Council ought not to be composed merely of

diplomatists. A diplomatist represents national prestige, and his credit among his *confrères* depends upon his skill in securing supposed advantages for his own nation. He focusses in his own person the spirit of rivalry between States which is the chief obstacle to internationalism. The mental atmosphere in which he lives is that of the eighteenth century, with its "Balance of Power" and other shibboleths. Classification by nations is only one way of classifying mankind, but the diplomatic machine ignores all other ways. The world of finance, the world of learning, the world of Socialism—to take only three examples—are international, each of great importance in its own way, each having certain interests which cut right across the divisions of States. If each nation appointed to the Council not only a diplomatist but also a financier, a representative of learning, and a champion of labour, there would often be cross-divisions, and the voting would not always be by nations. International interests, as opposed to merely national advantage, would have some chance of a hearing in such a Council, and it might occasionally happen that the welfare of civilisation would be the decisive consideration. Foreign policy has remained everywhere the exclusive domain of an aristocratic clique. What they have made of it, we see. It is time to secure a less ignorant and less prejudiced conduct of affairs by the admission of the democracy to an active administrative share.

The deliberations of the Council should be public and it should refuse to regard as binding any treaty, agreement, or understanding of which the terms had been kept secret. By means of secrecy, an air of mystery and hocus-pocus is preserved, of which the sole use and purpose is to keep power in official hands, and to prevent the intrusion of common sense into the arcana of diplomacy. The public is hoodwinked by the assurance that secrecy is essential to national security. Hitherto, on this plea, even the most democratic countries of Europe have handed over their destinies blindfold to men who have abused their trust by policies diametrically opposed to what their followers desired. Only publicity can prevent a repetition of this crime.

In urging that men who are not professional diplomatists ought to take part in the International Council, I am not wishing to suggest that diplomatists, as individuals, are any worse than other men, but only that their training, their traditions, their way of life, and the fact that they represent the national interest to the exclusion of all other considerations, must tend to close their minds to an order of ideas which lies outside the scope of their official duties. Even men who are wholly estimable in private life will be governed in their political ideas by the interest which they represent. The secretary of the Automobile Association—I speak hypothetically, since I do not know who he is—may be an ardent patriot, and anxious, as an individual, to bear his share of the expense of the Navy, but he will infallibly protest when it is proposed to put a tax on petrol. The editor of the *Licensed Victuallers' Gazette* may be a zealous temperance man in his private capacity, but as an editor he is bound to raise an outcry when any

fresh burden is placed upon ''The Trade.'' So a diplomatist may, during his holidays, be an international
pacifist, but in his working hours he will struggle
to obtain small advantages for his country, even by
threatening war if necessary. This is the inevitable
effect of the interest which he represents, and can only
be counteracted by men who represent interests which
conflict less with those of civilisation in general.

Should the powers of the Council include military
intervention for the enforcement of its awards? Very
strong arguments may be urged on both sides.

It is assumed that, when a dispute arises, the Council will at once invite the Powers concerned to submit
to its arbitration, and that, if one party expresses
willingness to abide by its award while the other does
not, it will throw whatever weight it possesses against
the intractable party. It should also have the power
of examining questions likely to cause disputes in the
future, and of suggesting such adjustments and com-
promises as may seem just. But if its authority is
flouted, shall it rely upon moral force alone, or shall
it have power to invoke the armed support of all those
neutrals which send delegates to it?

In favour of armed intervention, it may be urged
that otherwise the Council will be futile, and will
afford no security against an aggressive military
Power. It will therefore not allay panics, prevent
wars, or tend to diminish armaments. If, on the other
hand, neutrals can be relied upon to be willing to
threaten armed intervention, and if their intervention
would always secure an overwhelming preponderance
of force on one side, then the mere threat would be

sufficient, and actual war would be prevented.

But this argument involves many doubtful hypotheses, and is perhaps inspired less by a sober review of the facts than by the wish to find a short cut to universal peace. Unless almost all the Powers sincerely desire peace, an alliance among the more bellicose Powers might be strong enough to flout all the others, and in that case the only result of the Council would be to make the war world-wide. Also it is much to be feared that neutrals could not be trusted to intervene by force of arms in a dispute in which they had no interest beyond the desire to preserve the peace: the whole system would be in danger of breaking down just when it was most needed. The most pacific Powers—notably the United States— would probably refuse altogether to enter a system entailing such vast and manifold obligations. And within each nation, the necessity of being constantly prepared to go to war would run counter to the wishes of peaceful people, although it would be from such people that the scheme would have to derive its support, since its aim would be the revention of war. For these reasons, it does not seem desirable *at present* that the decisions of the International Council should be enforced by military intervention.

I do not think the decisions of the Council would have no weight if they rested upon moral force alone. The efforts made by both sides in the present war to persuade the United States of the justice of their cause show how much the sympathy of neutrals is valued, even when there is hardly a thought of their abandoning neutrality. And the mere existence of

an impartial tribunal, to which each side could yield
without loss of dignity, would in most cases suffice to
prevent the diplomatic deadlock which precedes war.
Public opinion, which at present has no means of
hearing any unbiassed statement, would be powerfully
influenced by an authoritative award, and the pacific
forces in the countries concerned could bring pressure
to bear on the government to bow to the decisions of
the Council. If the pacific forces were strong, this
pressure would probably be sufficient; if not, no system could make peace secure. For, in the last resort,
peace can only be preserved if public opinion desires
peace in most of the great nations.

(3) Far more important than any question of
machinery is the problem of producing in all civilised
nations such a horror of war that public opinion will
insist upon peaceful methods of settling disputes.
When this war ends, probably every nation in Europe
will feel such an intense weariness of the struggle that
no great war will be probable for another generation.
The problem is, so to alter men's standards and outlook that, when the weariness has passed away, they
shall not fall back into the old bad way, but shall
escape from the nightmare into a happier world of
free co-operation.

The first thing to make men realise is that modern
war is an absurdity as well as a crime, and that it can
no longer secure such national advantages as, for
example, England secured by the Seven Years' War.
After the present war, it should be easy to persuade
even the most ignorant and high-placed persons of this
truth.

But it is even more necessary to alter men's conceptions of "glory" and "patriotism." Beginning in childhood, with the school text-books of history, and continuing in the Press and in common talk, men are taught that the essence of "glory" is successful robbery and slaughter. The most "glorious" nation is the one which kills the greatest numbers of foreigners and seizes the greatest extent of foreign territory. The most "patriotic" citizen is the one who most strongly opposes any attempt at justice or mercy in his country's dealings with other countries, and who is least able to conceive of mankind as all one family, struggling painfully from a condition of universal strife towards a society where love of one's neighbor is no longer thought a crime. The division of the world into nations is a fact which must be accepted, but there is no reason to accept the narrow nationalism which envies the prosperity of others and imagines it a hindrance to our own progress. If a better and saner world is to grow out of the horror of futile carnage, men must learn to find their nation's glory in the victory of reason over brute instincts, and to feel the true patriotism which demands that our country should deserve admiration rather than extort fear. If this lesson can be taught to all, beginning with the children in the schools, we may hope for a lasting peace, and the machinery for securing it will grow out of the universal desire. So long as hate and fear and pride are praised and encouraged, war can never become an impossibility. But there is now, if men have the courage to use it, an awakening of heart and mind such as the world has never known before: men see that war is wicked and that war is foolish.  If the statesmen will play their part, by showing that war is not inevitable, there is hope that our children may live in a happier world, and look back upon us with the wondering pity of a wiser age.

# THE DANGER TO CIVILIZATION

In the eighteenth and nineteenth centuries, men commonly congratulated themselves that they lived in an era of enlightenment and progress, very far removed from the ignorance, superstition and barbarity of the dark ages. Progress in civilisation came to seem natural and certain, no longer needing deliberate effort for its realisation. Under the influence of a fancied security, men gradually came to value less consciously the effort after mental advancement. But history gives no justification for the sense of security, and the present war, to those who view it as an historical event, not simply as a vehicle for their own passions, affords grave reason for fear that the civilisation we have slowly built up is in danger of self-destruction. This aspect of the war has been too little considered on both sides, the fear of defeat and the longing for victory have made men oblivious of the common task of Europe and of the work which Europe had been performing for mankind at large. In all that has made the nations of the West important to the world, they run the risk of being involved in a common disaster, so great and so terrible that it will outweigh, to the historian in the future, all the penalties of military defeat and all the glories of military victory.

Over and over again, in the past, the greatest civilisations have been destroyed or degraded by war. The fighting which Homer has taught us to regard as glorious swept away the Mycenean civilization, which was succeeded by centuries of confused and barbarous conflict. The speech of Pericles to the Athenians at the beginning of the Peloponnesian war has been thought worthy of a place among recruiting appeals in the London Underground Railway; yet the war which he recommended by recalling the greatness of Athenian civilisation proved in fact to be its end, and Athenians born after the war added almost nothing to the world's permanent possessions. It is impossible to imagine a more sinister precedent than that war, in which the most fruitful and splendid civilisation the world has known was brought to an end for ever by pride of power and love of battle. The Roman civilisation which succeeded it, though less productive, might have seemed secure by its great extent, yet it perished almost completely in the barbarian invasion. The remnants out of which the modern world has grown were preserved, not by the men who fought against the barbarians, but by monks who retired from the strife and devoted their lives to religion. And in more modern times, the Thirty Years' War had an influence, impossible to overestimate, in brutalising the German character and making the level of humane feeling lower than that of nations less subject to the degrading influence of invasion and rapine.

When we consider the world in a broad historical retrospect, it is what nations have added to civilisation that makes us permanently honour them, not what they have achieved in conquest and dominion. Great conquerors, such as Attila, Timur and Zenghis

Khan, trample across the pages of history full of noise and fury, signifying nothing: like an earthquake or a plague, they come and pass, leaving only a record of destruction and death. The Jews and Greeks, the Romans, and the modern nations of Western Europe, have contributed almost everything that has been added in historical times to creation and diffusion of what is permanently valuable in human life. The Romans spread throughout their Empire what had been created by the Jews in religion, by the Greeks in art and science; on this foundation, after a long interval of barbarism, the Italians, the French, the English and the Germans built the world in which we have hitherto lived. The progress in which we have rejoiced has not grown up by itself: it has been created and sustained by individual and collective effort. What great men have done in literature, in art, in natural knowledge, has been made available to large numbers by education. Private violence has been suppressed; the rudiments of learning have become more and more accessible to all classes; and mental activity has been continually stimulated and broadened as the progress of science liberated more and more men from the need of manual labour.

It is this achievement, imperfect as it has hitherto been, which chiefly entitles the Western nations to respect. It is the furtherance of civilisation which makes us admire the Roman Empire more than that of Xerxes, or the British Empire more than that of China. It is this service to mankind that is being jeopardised by the present war. Whether, when it ends, the English, the French, or the Germans will still have the energy and will to carry on the progress of the past, is a very doubtful question, depending chiefly upon the length of the war and the spirit fostered by the settlement. Of all the reasons for desiring an early peace, this is, to my mind, the strongest. The danger, great and pressing as I believe it to be, is obscured amid the clash of national ambitions, because it requires us to fix our attention on individuals, not on States. There is some risk of forgetting the good of individuals under the stress of danger to the State: yet, in the long run, the good of the State cannot be secured if the individuals have lost their vigor. In what follows, I shall ignore political issues, and speak only of the effect on separate men and women and young people; but a corresponding effect on the State must follow in the end, since the State lives only by the life of its separate citizens.

This war, to begin with, is worse than any previous war in the direct effect upon those who fight. The armies are far larger than they have ever been before, and the loss by death or permanent disablement immensely exceeds what has occurred in the past.* The losses are enhanced by the deadlock, which renders a purely strategical decision of the war almost impossible. We are told to regard it as a war of attrition, which means presumably that victory is hoped from the gradual extermination of the German armies. Our military authorities, apparently,

---

*According to Mr. Balfour, Great Britain, which has suffered far less than France, Russia, Germany or Austria-Hungary, has had more casualties in the first year than Germany had in the war of 1870.

contemplate with equanimity a three years' war, ending only by our excess of population: when practically all Germans of military age have been killed
or maimed, it is thought that there will still remain
a good many English, Russians, and Italians, and
perhaps a sprinkling of Frenchmen. But in the
course of such destruction almost all that makes the
Allied nations worth defending will have been lost:
the enfeebled, impoverished remnants will lack the
energy to resume the national life which existed before the war, and the new generation will grow up
listless under the shadow of a great despair. I hope
that the men in authority are wiser than their words;
but everything that has been said points to this result as what is intended by those who control our
fate.

The actual casualties represent only a small part
of the real loss in the fighting. In former wars,
seasoned veterans made the best soldiers, and men
turned from the battlefield with their physical and
mental vigour unimpaired. In this war, chiefly owing to the nerve-shattering effect of shell-fire and continual noise, this is no longer the case. All troops
gradually deteriorate at the front: the best troops
are those who are fresh, provided they are adequately
trained. In all the armies, a number of men go mad,
a much larger number suffer from nervous collapse,
becoming temporarily blind or dumb or incapable of
any effort of will and almost all suffer considerable
nervous injury, causing loss of vitality, energy, and
power of decision. In great part, no doubt, this effect
is temporary; but there is no reason to think that

in most men something of it will be permanent, and
in not a few the nervous collapse will remain very
serious.  I fear it must be assumed that almost all
who have seen much fighting will have grown incapable of great effort, and will only be able, at best,
to slip unobtrusively through the remaining years
of life.  Since the fighting will, if the war lasts much
longer, absorb the bulk of the male population of
Europe between 18 and 45, this cause alone will
make it all but impossible to maintain and hand on
the tradition of civilisation which has been slowly
acquired by the efforts of our ancestors.

We are told by advocates of war that its moral
effects are admirable; on this ground, they say, we
ought to be thankful that there is little prospect of an
end to wars.  The men who repeat this hoary falsehood must have learnt nothing from the reports of
friends returned from the war, and must have refrained from talking with wounded soldiers in hospital and elsewhere.  It is true that, in those who
enlist of their own free will, there is a self-devotion
to the cause of their country which deserves all
praises; and their first experience of warfare often
gives them a horror of its futile cruelty which makes
them for a time humane and ardent friends of peace.
If the war had lasted only three months, these good
effects might have been its most important moral
consequences.  But as the months at the front pass
slowly by, the first impulse is followed by quite
other moods.  Heroism is succeeded by a merely
habitual disregard of danger, enthusiasm for the national cause is replaced by passive obedience to orders.

Familiarity with horrors makes war seem natural, not the abomination which it is seen to be at first. Humane feeling decays, since, if it survived, no man could endure the daily shocks. In every army, reports of enemy atrocities, true or false, stimulate ferocity, and produce a savage thirst for reprisals. On the Western front at least, both sides have long ceased to take prisoners except in large batches. Our newspapers have been full of the atrocities perpetrated by German soldiers. Whoever listens to the conversation of wounded soldiers returned from the front will find that, in all the armies, some men become guilty of astonishing acts of ferocity. Will even the most hardened moralist dare to say that such men are morally the better for their experience of war? If the war had not occurred, they would probably have gone through life without ever having the wild beast in them aroused. There is a wild beast slumbering in almost every man, but civilised men know that it must not be allowed to awake. A civilised man who has once been under the domain of the wild beast has lost his moral self respect, his integrity and uprightness: a secret shame makes him cynical and despairing, without the courage that sees facts as they are, without the hope that makes them better. War is perpetrating this moral murder in the souls of vast millions of combatants; every day many are passing over to the dominion of the brute by acts which kill what is best within them. Yet, still our newspapers, parsons, and professors prate of the ennobling influence of war.

The war, hitherto, has steadily increased in ferocity,

and has generated a spirit of hatred in the armies which was absent in the early months. If it lasts much longer, we may be sure that it will grow still worse in these respects. The Germans, hitherto, have prospered, but if the tide turns, it is to be feared that their "frightfulness" in the past will be child's play compared with what will happen when they begin to anticipate defeat. They have already aroused among the Allies a hatred which is the greatest danger that now menaces civilisation; but if the war lasts much longer, and if the Germans are driven by fear into even greater crimes against humanity than they have hitherto committed, it is to be expected that a blind fury of destruction will drive us on and on until the good and evil of the old world have perished together in universal ruin. For this reason, if for no other, it is of the last importance to control hatred, to realise that almost all that is detestable in the enemy is the result of war, is brought out by war, in a greater or less degree, on our side as well as on the other, and will cease with the conclusion of peace but not before. If the terrible deeds that are done in the war are merely used to stimulate mutual hatred, they lead only to more war and to still more terrible deeds: along that road, there is no goal but exhaustion. If universal exhaustion is to be avoided, we must, sooner or later, forget our resentment, and remember that the war, whatever its outcome, is destroying on both sides the heritage of civilisation which was transmitted to us by our fathers and which it is our duty to hand on to our children as little impaired as possible.

When the war is over, the men who have taken part in it will not easily find their place again among the occupations of peace. They will have become accustomed to act under the strong stimulus of danger, or in mere obedience to orders; and they will be physically and mentally exhausted by the terrible strain of life in the trenches. For both reasons, they will have little will-power, little capacity for self-direction. It will be hardly possible to find room for them all in the labour market, and the first impulses of patriotism in their favour will probably soon die down. We cannot hope that very many of them will ever again be as useful citizens as they would have been if the war had not occurred. The habit of violence, once acquired, however legitimately, is not easily set aside, and the respect for law and order is likely to be much less after the war than it was before. If this state of mind concurs, as is likely, with serious distress and labour troubles ruthlessly repressed by a government grown used to autocratic power, the effect upon the national life will be disastrous and profound.

In the minds of most men on both sides, the strongest argument for prolonging the war is that no other course will secure us against its recurrence in the near future. In the opinion of Englishmen and German alike, their enemies have such a thirst for war that only their utter overthrow can secure the peace of the world. We are an essentially peace-loving nation—so both contend—and if we had the power, we should prevent such a war as this from occurring again. On this ground, it is urged by both that the

war must continue, since both believe that their own
side will ultimately be completely victorious.

I believe that in this both sides are profoundly
mistaken. I shall not discuss the question from a
political point of view, though I believe the political
argument is overwhelming. What I wish to urge is
the effect of war upon the imaginative outlook of men,
upon their standard of international conduct, and
upon the way in which they view foreign nations.
Individual passions and expectations in ordinary
citizens are at least as potent as the acts of governments in causing or averting wars, and in the long
run it is upon them that the preservation of peace
in future will depend. It is commonly said that
punishment will have an effect that nothing else can
have in turning the thoughts of our enemies away
from war and making them henceforth willing to
keep the peace. This argument assumes, quite falsely,
that men and nations are guided by self-interest in
their actions. Unfortunately this is not the case,
and the motives which do guide them are often worse
than self-interest. It is as clear as noonday that
no one of the nations involved in the present war
would have fought if self-interest had been its principle of action. Pride, prestige, love of dominion,
unwillingness to yield a triumph to others or to be-
have in a way which would be thought dishonourable,
these are among the motives which produced the war.
Each motive, no doubt, wove a myth of self-interest
about it, since people do not wish to think their
actions harmful to their own interests; but if self-
interest had been genuinely operative, the nations

would have made friends and co-operated in the works of peace. And if self-interest has not prevented this war, why should we expect that it will prevent future wars? Yet it is only by an appeal to self-interest that punishment can hope to be effective.

It is peace, not war, that in the long run turns men's thoughts away from fighting. No doubt when a great war ends there is a weariness which ensures a number of years of peace and recuperation; however this war may end, and, if it ended tomorrow, no matter on what terms, it would not break out again at once, because the impulse to war is exhausted for the moment. But for the future every additional month of war increases the danger, since it makes men increasingly view war as a natural condition of the world, renders them more and more callous to its horrors and to the loss of friends, and fills their imagination, especially the imagination of those who are now young, with war as something to be expected and with the thought that some foreign nations are so wicked as to make it our duty to destroy them.

If the war is brought to an end by reason, by a realisation on all sides that it is an evil, it may be possible to combat the imaginative outlook which it is engendering and to bring about an effective will to peace. But if only exhaustion ends the war, any revival of energy may lead to its renewal, especially if the positive ideals which make for peace have perished meanwhile in the universal death of all humane and civilised aspirations.

Through the effects of the war upon education, the mental calibre of the next generation is almost certain to be considerably lower than that of generations educated before the war. Education, from the highest to the lowest, is in constant danger of becoming a mere mechanical drill in which the young are taught to perform certain tasks in the way that is considered correct, and to believe that all intellectual questions have been decided once for all in the sense declared by the text-books. The education inspired by this spirit destroys the mental activity of the young, makes them passive in thought and active only in pursuing some humdrum ambition. It is this spirit which is the most insidious enemy of progress in an old civilisation, since it inculcates constantly, with a great parade of knowledge and authority, a Byzantine attitude of superstitious respect for what has been done and contempt for the credit of what is attempted in our own day. The mental life of Europe has only been saved from complete subjection to this spirit by a small percentage of teachers, more full of vitality than most, and more filled with a genuine delight in mental activity. These men are to be found almost exclusively among the younger teachers, the men whose hopes have not yet faded, who have not yet become the slaves of habit, who have enough spring of life to take lightly the weariness and expense of spirit in their daily task. It is this comparatively small number of teachers who keep alive the mental vigour that leads to new discoveries and new methods of dealing with old problems. Without them, there would be no progress; and without progress, we could not even stand still. What is known bears now such a large proportion to what our own age can hope to discover that the danger of traditionalism is very great; indeed it has only been averted by the continual triumph of the men of science.

After the war, the number of teachers with any power of stimulating mental life must be enormously diminished. Many of the younger teachers will have been killed, many others incapacitated; of those who remain, most will have lost hope and energy. For a number of years, teaching will be much more in the hands of the old and middle-aged, while those teachers who are still young in years will have lost much of the spirit of youth in the strain of the war. The result will be that the new generation will have less expectation of progress than its predecessors, less power of bearing lightly the burden of knowledge. It is only a small stock of very unusual energy that makes mental progress; and that small stock is being wasted on the battle-field.

What is true in the purely intellectual sphere is equally true in art and literature and all the creative activities of our civilisation. In all these, if the war lasts long, it is to be expected that the great age of Europe will be past and that men will look back to the period now coming to an end as the later Greeks looked back to the age of Pericles. Who then is supreme in Europe will be a matter of no importance to mankind; in the madness of rivalry, Europe will have decreed its own insignificance.

All the difficulties of restoring civilisation when the present outburst of barbarism has passed will be increased by economic exhaustion. Hitherto, in England, most men have hardly begun to feel the economic effects of the war, and if peace were to come this autumn it is possible that the economic effects in this country would not be very profound or very disastrous. But if the war drags on after the period of easy borrowing is past, great and general impoverishment must result. Those who still have capital will be able to exact a continually increasing rate of interest; probably it will become necessary to borrow largely in America, and the interest will represent a perpetual tribute which Europe will have to pay to America as the price of its indulgence in war.

The enormous production of munitions will either cease suddenly with a violent dislocation of the labour market, or will be continued out of deference to vested interests, causing a constant stimulus to new wars and to mutual suspicions and fears on the part of the rival states. The reabsorption of the men who have been fighting will be difficult, especially as their places will have been largely taken by women at lower wages, and casualties will have increased the number of widows and single women anxious to earn their own living. The men who return from the front will have grown accustomed to a higher standard in food than that of the ordinary workingman, and will feel themselves heroes; both causes will make it difficult for them to settle down to a poorer living than they had before the war, yet it is almost certain that that is what they will have to do. The Government, having grown accustomed to almost absolute power during the war, having unlimited soldiers under its orders, and having no organized opposition to fear, will be far more ruthless than it has hitherto been in suppressing strikes and enforcing submission. This will probably lead to much revolutionary feeling, without the energy or the ability that could make revolution successful.

In these circumstances, there will be little money available for education or the promotion of art and science. In order to be able still to keep up huge armaments, the governing classes will diminish expenditure on the objects they consider least important; among these, education is sure to be included. Their object will be to produce a proletariat unskilled in everything except shooting and drill, docile through ignorance and formidable through military discipline. This must result in either apathy or civil war. Unless the war ends soon, it is apathy that will result; but in either event, our civilisation is imperiled.

There are some who hold that the war will result in a permanent increase in the rate of wages. But there are several broad grounds for thinking that this view is mistaken. To begin with, many young and vigorous workers will have been killed or disabled in the war, and the population will contain a larger proportion than before of old men, women and children. The more productive sections of the population will be diminished, and the production of goods per head will be less than it was when the war broke out. As there will be less to divide, some one must suffer. The capitalist is not likely to suffer, since the demands of war enable him to secure a good rate of interest now, and the reconstruction of what the war has destroyed will cause a great demand for capital for some time after the war. It is unlikely that the land-owner will suffer, since he will be able to impose tariffs on the plea of revenue and protection against German competition. It seems inevitable that the loss must fall upon wage-earners. In bringing about this loss, capitalists will find the growth of cheap female labour during the war a great help, and this opportunity will be improved by the enormous numbers of discharged soldiers and munitions workers seeking employment. I do not see how this situation can result otherwise than in a great fall of wages.

To sum up: the bad results which we have been considering do not depend upon the question of victory or defeat: they will fall upon all the nations, and their severity depends only upon the length and destructiveness of the war. If the war lasts much longer, very few healthy men of military age will have failed to be injured physically to a greater or less extent in any of the nations involved; the moral level everywhere will be lowered by familiarity with horrors, leading, in most men, to an easy acquiescence; the mental efficiency of Europe will be greatly diminished by the inevitable deterioration of education and by the death or nervous weakening of many of the best minds among the young; and the struggle for life will almost certainly become more severe among all classes except the idle rich. The collective life of Europe, which has carried it on since the Renaissance in the most wonderful upward movement known to history, will have received a wound which may well prove mortal. If the war does not come to an end soon, it is to be feared that we are at the end of a great epoch, and that the future of Europe will not be on a level with its past.

Is there any conceivable gain from the continuation of the war to be set against this loss? It is difficult to imagine any gain which could outweigh so terrible a loss, and none of the gains which are suggested can compare with it for a moment. But in fact even the gains which are suggested are illusory. It is fairly clear now that neither side can hope for the absolute and crushing victory which both expected at the outset, except at a cost which cannot be seriously contemplated. Sooner or later, negotiation will have to end the war. The claims of Belgium, which are for us an obligation of honour, will, it is known, be recognised by Germany in return for compensations elsewhere.* The argument that, if we do not crush Germany, we cannot be safe from a recurrence of the present war in the near future, is probably the one that carries most weight. But in fact it will not bear a moment's examination. In the first place, most military authorities are agreed that it is impossible to crush Germany. In the second place, there have been wars before in which Germany was not our enemy, and there may be such wars in future: unless the spirit of rivalry is checked, the removal of one rival is only the prelude to the growth of another. In the third place, if the war lasts much longer we shall incur now all the evils which we might incur in the future if the war broke out again, and the present evils are certain while the future war is open

---

*See e. g. "The Times", Sept. 4, 1915.

to doubt. Germany has suffered appalling losses, and is in a very different mood from that in which it began the war, as may be seen by the growing condemnation of the Hymn of Hate. A peace now, giving no definite victory to either side, would probably leave Germany, for many years, determined not to go to war again; and no peace can insure us against wars a generation hence. In continuing the war, we are incurring great and certain evils for a very doubtful gain. The obligation of honour towards Belgium is more fully discharged if the Germans are led to evacuate Belgium by negotiation than if they are driven out at the cost of destroying whatever they have left unharmed. Both on their side and on ours, the real motive which prolongs the war is pride. Is there no statesman who can think in terms of Europe, not only of separate nations? Is our civilisation a thing of no account to all our rulers? I hope not. I hope that somewhere among the men who hold power in Europe there is at least one who will remember, at this late date, that we are the guardians, not only of the nation, but of that common heritage of thought and art and a humane way of life into which we were born, but which our children may find wasted by our blind violence and hate.

# THE ENTENTE POLICY, 1904-1915
## A Reply to Professor Gilbert Murray.

### I. Introduction.

There are some among us who hold that, if our foreign policy in recent years had been conducted with more courage, more openness, and more idealism, there is a likelihood that the present European War would never have occurred. In holding this view, we are in no way concerned to defend the German Government; it is clear, at least to me, that the German Government is much more to blame than our own, both for the outbreak of war and for the way in which the war has been conducted. But Germany's guilt is no proof of our innocence. And if we remain to the end wrapped in self-righteousness, impervious to facts which are not wholly creditable to us, we shall, in the years after the war, merely repeat the errors of the past, and find ourselves, in the end, involved in other wars as terrible and destructive as the one which we are now waging.

The criticism of British foreign policy which seems to us necessary is not a personal criticism of Sir Edward Grey: he has been merely the instrument, the man who carried on an ancient tradition. I cannot discover any matter, great or small, in which the policy of the Foreign Office was different under his administration and under Lord Lansdowne's.* It is not the man, but the maxims which he has inherited, that must be criticised.

*South African affairs, mentioned by Professor Murray, are not under the Foreign Office.

Professor Gilbert Murray, under the tutelage of the Foreign Office, has written an elaborate defence of Sir Edward Grey.* In criticising Professor Murray, I shall not be concerned with Sir Edward Grey's personality, but merely with the policy which he inherited and developed.

Before embarking upon the history of British foreign policy, Professor Murray begins by a very misleading description of the state of mind of those whom he calls ''pro-Germans'', among whom he instances Mr. Brailsford and myself. They are, he says, ''often very clever'', but ''not at present in a state of mind which enables them to see or even to seek the truth.'' ''The Pro-Germans''—he says—''are in a very small minority and have to fight hard. And many of them become so wrapped up in their own immediate controversy that, as far as their combative feelings are concerned, the central enemy of the human race is Sir Edward Grey; next to him come the British Cabinet and the most popular generals. The Kaiser is to them a prisoner in the dock, a romantic unfortunate, to be defended against overwhelming odds. It needs great strength of mind for a member of a small fighting minority, like this, to be even moderately fair in controversy.''

Perhaps it does require some strength of mind, even to belong to so small a minority; but whatever strength of mind is required to be ''even moderately fair'' when one belongs to a great fighting majority has been denied to Professor Murray. He has fallen

*The Foreign Policy of Sir Edward Grey, 1906-15, by Gilbert Murray.   Clarendon Press 1-6d.

into the absurd assumption—which no man makes in the private quarrels in which he is not personally involved—that if one side is to blame, the other must be innocent.

As for the "central enemy of the human race", that is a melodramatic conception: most Germans, apparently, regard Sir Edward Grey in this light, while Professor Murray, like most Englishmen, regards the Kaiser in this light. Those whom he attacks as not "even moderately fair", protest against such sensationalism. We perceive that in previous wars similar views have been held on each side, to be unanimously discarded by subsequent historians; and we do not believe that what has always been false before has now suddenly become true. If we seem to emphasise the faults on our side, that is because they are ignored by our compatriots; if we seem to say little about the faults on the other side, that is because every newspaper and professor throughout the country is making them known. Moreover it is more profitable to be conscious of our own faults than of the faults of our enemies: we can amend our own faults if we become aware of them, whereas we only increase hatred on both sides by proclaiming the faults of the enemy. As for the Kaiser, ever since I first began to know Germany, 20 years ago, I have abominated him; I have consistently regarded him, and I now regard him, as one of the sources of evil in the world; and in what I have written on the war there is not a word or a syllable which could be construed, by any ingenuity, into a defence of the Kaiser. But if Professor Murray were "even moderately fair in controversy", he would perceive that the Kaiser's guilt cannot alone suffice to establish the immaculate sinlessness of our Foreign Office.

With the whole of what Professor Murray says as to the wickedness of Germany's invasion of Belgium I am in complete agreement. But except the pleasure derived from denunciation, no good is achieved by dwelling upon the sins of our enemies, since they very naturally pay no attention to our opinions, while we become puffed up with self-righteousness. In the opinion that Mr. Brailsford and 1 ''are not at present in a state of mind which enables them to see or even to seek the truth'', Professor Murray will find unanimous agreement throughout Europe, not excepting Germany, Austria and Turkey. My pamphlet, which he regards as pro-German, has, I am informed, been prohibited in Austria* on the ground of the vehemence of its pro-English bias. It is a comfort in these times to find any matter upon which all the warring nations are agreed. The sinfulness of impartiality is such a matter, and to have brought out this fundamental agreement is perhaps as great a reward as we can hope for.

When the war broke out, the view taken by most Liberals in England was that our participation was due to the German violation of Belgium and our obligations under the treaty of 1839. This was not the opinion of Unionists: it was repeatedly combated by ''The Times'' (see especially the leading article of March 8, 1915; see also Spectator, Dec. 19, 1914) and

---

*But not apparently in Hungary. See "Morning Post', Sep. 25, 1915.

Belgium was not mentioned in the official Unionist communication of August 2,* a promising support to the Government if they took part in the war. Fortunately it was not the view taken by France and Russia; unfortunately it was not the view taken by Germany. Professor Murray does not commit himself fully: he speaks of the German attack on Belgium as "one of the obvious and important events leading up to the war." This phrase is vague. But I do not think there can now be two opinions as to the part played by Belgium in our participation: if the Germans had not attacked Belgium, there would have been more resignations in the Cabinet and less unanimity of public opinion, but the Government would have found it impossible to stand aside while France was being crushed. France, not Belgium, was for us the decisive factor. But as Professor Murray seems anxious to suggest a doubt on this point, let us see what the evidence is.

The German Ambassador asked Sir Edward Grey whether he could promise neutrality if not only the integrity and independence of France (including colonies), but also the neutrality of Belgium, were respected. Sir Edward Grey replied that he could give no such promise. (White Paper, No. 123.) On this Professor Murray comments as follows:

---

*The following is the text of Mr. Bonar Law's letter to Mr. Asquith, of Aug. 2, 1914:

Dear Mr. Asquith, Lord Lansdowne and I feel it our duty to inform you that, in our opinion as well as in that of all the colleagues whom we have been able to consult, it would be fatal to the honour and security of the United Kingdom to hesitate in supporting France and Russia at the present juncture; and we offer our unhesitating support to the Government in any measures they may consider necessary for that object.

Yours very truly, A. Bonar Law.

"If Germany, from whatever motive, chose to use the Austro-Serbian dispute as an occasion for making war on France, then we must have our hands free. We could not tell Germany how much we would take to stand aside while France was crushed.* We could not arrange with Germany for a limited crushing of France. . . . All such bargaining was both dishonourable and illusory and dangerous."

That is to say, honour or interest, or both, so bound us to France that we could not, even to save Belgium from invasion, stand aside while France was attacked. So far from Belgium being the cause of our intervention, we were precluded from making any effective diplomatic attempt to protect Belgium by the fact that we could not promise neutrality even if Belgium were respected. In this the situation differed from that of 1870, when Belgium was, for us, the decisive factor, and was, consequently, efficiently protected by our diplomacy. Professor Murray, who maintains that we did not know that Germany would invade Belgium, cannot reply that we were certain in advance of the fruitlessness of such a policy from the Belgian point of view.

Before the question of Belgium had arisen, on August 2, we had already promised France to intervene if the German Navy attacked the Northern or Western coasts of France. (This was an obligation of

*So far is this from being a correct statement of the case that even at the eleventh hour Germany snatched at the chance of France remaining neutral, which seemed to be presented owing to a misunderstanding. See telegrams published by Norddeutsche Allgemeine Zeitung, Aug. 20, 1914, Sept. 5, 1914, quoted on pp. 256, 258 of Price's "Diplomatic History of the War." See also Sir E. Grey's reply in House of Commons to Lord R. Cecil, Aug. 28, 1914.

honour, resulting from the fact that, as a consequence of our military and naval conversations with
the French, their Navy had been withdrawn from the
Mediterranean, leaving their Channel and Atlantic
coasts only protected by our ships.)  In Sir E. Grey's
speech of August 3, Belgium forms only a small
part of his case; and in his later speeches it was chiefly
France that he spoke of.  He always made it plain,
both in his speeches and in the despatches in the
White Paper, that in his view we were bound to
come to the help of France.  And of any supporter
of the war is asked: "Would you have been prepared to stand aside while France was crushed?"  he
is all but certain to answer that he would not.  Belgium showed Germany at its worst, but it did not
show us at our best.  It gave Germany an occasion
for brutal violence; it gave our Foreign Office an
occasion for hypocrisy.

Not only should we have taken part in the war if
Belgium had not been involved, but if our national
interests had been on the side of Germany we should
not have taken part, even though the Germans had
violated Belgium.  In 1887, there was severe tension between France and Germany and war was expected.  The likelihood of the Germans marching
through Belgium was admitted, and prominent newspapers of both parties discussed our obligations in
case that should happen.*  The conclusion they came
to was that we need not regard our obligation as requiring us to go to war.  Yet our obligation then,

---

*Cf. "Standard", Feb. 4, 1887; "Pall Mall Gazette" (at that
time Liberal), Feb. 4 and 5, 1887; "Spectator", Feb. 5, 1887.
What these newspapers said is given in Appendix A.

whatever its nature, was precisely the same as in 1914, since it rested wholly on the treaty of 1839. What then had changed in the interval? Our view of British interests had changed, and nothing else. In 1887, we had quarrels with France and Russia, but no quarrel with Germany; our leaning was towards the Triple Alliance, and in a European War we should have hoped for the victory of Germany. That is why we then made light of our obligation to Belgium. And in 1914 we made much of our obligation to Belgium because we were against Germany. So far at least as our Foreign Office is concerned, to say that we were against Germany because we were for Belgium is to invert cause and effect; the truth is that we were for Belgium because we were against Germany.

It was clearly the desire and intention of the Foreign Office to support France in the event of a war between France and Germany. But no formal alliance could be concluded, because it was very doubtful whether Liberal and Radical opinion would, in quiet times, support the Government if it attempted to make such an alliance. Most Englishmen now are of opinion that the Government was wiser than its doubtful supporters; like Professor Murray, they hold that criticism which formerly seemed justified has been proved by Germany to have been ill-founded. This misses the point of the criticism. Almost all the critics had long believed in the existence of a powerful war-party in Germany, and in a wide-spread intention to use the German Navy for aggressive purposes. Criticism of our foreign policy does not rest upon denial of these now obvious facts; it rests upon the fact that our foreign policy strengthened the war party in Germany, made the task of German friends of peace an impossible one, and supported France and Russia in enterprises which were inherently indefensible. While German policy was still doubtful, while there was still a considerable chance that aggressive tendencies might be held in check, we, by our hostility, roused the combativeness and national pride of the Germans, and fostered the belief that they could only escape defeat by aggression. And it was this belief which precipitated the war.

A candid defender of our foreign policy might, I think, state the case somewhat as follows:

"During the Boer War, we were faced with the unanimous ill-will of Europe, and for some months there was grave danger lest France, Germany and Russia should combine against us. This danger was averted, partly by the unappeasable hostility of France to Germany, partly by the fact that the combined navies of France, Germany and Russia were at that time hardly a match for the British Navy. With the German Navy Laws of 1898 and 1900, however, it became clear that we were entering upon a new epoch: we could no longer hope to be superior at sea to a combination of all the continental Powers. It became necessary to have friends on the Continent, in order to avoid the risk of a coalition against us. We had offered our friendship to Germany, through the medium of Mr. Joseph Chamberlain,* but this offer had been refused.** Germany's refusal, taken

---

*Mr. Chamberlain's Birmingham speech, May 13, 1898.
**See Bülow, Imperial Germany, pp. 31 ff, for grounds of Germany's rejection.

in conjunction with the German Navy Law of 1900, made us believe that Germany was aiming at naval supremacy, and forced us to seek the friendship of France and Russia. As soon as the Boer War was ended, we began negotiations with France to settle outstanding questions, and in 1904, we concluded the Anglo-French Entente, in which we promised to support the French claim to Morocco in return for French recognition of our position in Egypt. Somewhat parodoxically, the conclusion of the Entente was facilitated by recollection of the Fashoda incident, which had shown the French that their colonial expansion could not be effected in opposition to Great Britain.

"The conclusion of the Entente with Russia was a more difficult matter. For the protection of our interests in India and the Far East, we had allied ourselves in 1902 with Japan, which, under the shelter of the alliance, was able successfully to resist Russia in the war of 1904-5. This war produced great tension in our relations with Russia, and would probably have led to hostilities through the Dogger Bank incident, but for our Entente with France and the hope of an Entente with Russia. In the end, the Russo-Japanese war, like Fashoda, facilitated our new policy, since it showed Russia the difficulty of succeeding in opposition to us. As soon as the war was ended, we effectively reconciled Russia and Japan, joined France in providing a much-needed loan for the Russian Government, and by the partition of Persia enabled Russia to secure peacefully a long-desired object which we should formerly have opposed by force of arms. In this way our friendship with France and Russia was cemented by mutual advantage.

"In this situation, we might reasonably hope that Germany would hesitate to attack so strong a group as the Triple Entente, and at first everything seemed to encourage our hopes. Germany's Bagdad Railway scheme lingered on in a state of suspended animation, smothered in the complications of international finance. The French claim to Morocco, which we had been unable to sustain during the Russo-Japanese war, was successfully asserted in 1911, though Germany's face was saved by compensation in the Cameroons. Russia, being satisfied in Persia and definitely thwarted in the Far East, turned its attention to the Balkans, where Germany had to submit to the defeat, first of Turkey, then of Bulgaria, in the two Balkan wars. Owing to German friendship with the Turk, the Tripoli war definitely estranged Italy from the Central Empires. In all these respects our policy was successful. Soon, owing to the Three Years' Service Law in France, the reorganisation of the Russian army, and the projected strategic railways in Poland, the position of the Triple Entente would have been unassailable. But at this moment the Austrian attack on Serbia came as a challenge to the Triple Entente; Russia's prestige precluded surrender, and, though the moment was inopportune, the war was felt to be unavoidable."

An equally candid defender of German foreign policy, with exactly the same national aspirations as those which inspire our diplomatists, would view the same series of events in quite a different way. His reply would be something like this:

"Germany has been growing rapidly in population, in wealth, and in trade; more and more, the livelihood of Germans is becoming dependent upon the Open Door, the power of exporting manufactures, and security for imports of food. France, whose population and trade are stationary, has a Colonial Empire four times as great as ours. Austria-Hungary and Turkey, our only friends, are threatened with disruption by the revolutionary activity and the ruthless warfare of the South Slavs, protected and favoured by Russia. England, by its Navy, can at any moment cut off part of our food-supply and strangle our trade. We have tried every means of escaping from this situation without war, but in vain. In 1905, we asked that the status of Morocco, which had been decided by an international agreement (the Madrid Convention of 1880), should only be altered by a new international agreement. In spite of the obvious justice of our demand, England and France opposed us, and yielded only to the threat of force. At the resulting Algeciras Conference, we submitted to the asquisition of special rights by France and Spain, although at that time (when Russia was occupied in Manchuria) there could be no doubt that the preponderance of force was on our side.

"France secured a free hand for the Moroccan adventure by acknowledging the British position in Egypt, by withdrawing opposition to Italian ambitions in Tripoli, and by giving the Mediterranean coast of Morocco to Spain. When at last it became clear that France meant to occupy Morocco, we demanded that, in justice, we, like England, Italy and Spain, should receive some compensation for our acquiescence. In this demand, also, it was only by threatening war that we succeeded, and then very inadequately. In Mesopotamia, we discovered a country capable of great fertility, but rendered barren by misgovernment. Here again, our plans were thwarted by the opposition of England, Russia's initial opposition being withdrawn after the Potsdam Agreement of 1910. The Tripoli war and the two Balkan Wars, of which we remained merely spectators, were all decided in a way inimical to our interests. At last it became clear that the ambitions of the Triple Entente must prosper at Germany's expense so long as peace was preserved among the Great Powers, and that the precisely similar ambitions of Germany could never prosper except by the use of our incomparable army. If we had remained longer inactive, the strengthening of Russia and the growth of the South Slavs would have rendered us powerless, and we should have been unable to obtain the share of the Empire which is our due. Our love of peace has been proved during the last forty-four years; only the intolerable policy of encirclement has at last compelled us to draw the sword.''

This imaginary speech does not, of course, represent my own views, any more than the speech which I put into the mouth of a defender of our policy. The two speeches are merely intended to represent the best that can be said for the two policies without actual denial of plain facts. I have presented our

case and that of Germany without the moral indignation in which they are usually clothed. Germans,
to account for the Navy Law of 1900, will point
out how they longed, in 1899, to come to the rescue
of gallant little South Africa, when we committed
what was regarded as an international crime, the reasons for so regarding it being, as Professor Murray
quaintly says, "perhaps four".* Germans will say
that their inability to succour the oppressed on
that occasion, their incapacity to defend right
against might and democracy against militarism, first
showed them that they must have a navy if justice
was to prevail in the world and small nations were
to be safe from their big neighbours. All this is of
course hypocrisy on their part, and I have omitted
it from the statement of their case. If there seem to
be any omissions in the statement of our case, the
motive is the same.

Stripped of parliamentary verbiage, the fundamental fact about the European situation is that all
the Great Powers of Europe have precisely the same
objects: territory, trade and prestige. In pursuit of
these objects no one of the Great Powers shrinks from
wanton aggression, war and chicanery. But owing
to the geographical position of Germany and our
naval supremacy, England can achieve all its purposes by wars outside Europe, whereas English and
Russian policy has shown that Germany cannot
achieve its aims except by a European war. We have

---

*"Most decently-informed people in almost every region of the
world regard the German attack on Belgium. . . . . with vivid
indignation as a obvious international crime. The reasons for so
regarding it are perhaps four." Murray, p. 6.

made small wars because small wars were what suited our purpose; Germany has made a great war because a great war was what suited Germany's purpose. We and they alike have been immoral in aim and brutal in method, each in the exact degree which was thought to be to the national advantage. If either they or we had had loftier aims or less brutal methods, the war might have been avoided. As far as they are concerned, English readers will admit this at once; it is my object in what follows to prove that it is equally true of the Entente.

## II. MOROCCO.

The influence of the Moroccan question in stimulating warlike feeling both in Germany and in France is little appreciated in this country, and could certainly not be discovered from Professor Murray's account. An Italian learned journal, "Scientia," has invited articles by learned men of all countries, and the Editor has finally summed up his own editorial conclusions. On the subject of Morocco, the Editor says ("Scientia," June-July, 1915, pp. 44, 45).

"The first tangible result of the Triple Entente as it affected Germany was her complete and definite exclusion, at the risk, twice occurring, of a European War, from Morocco.......This exclusion was perhaps an error for the cause of European peace, because of the great disappointment and the lively invitation which the incident left throughout Germany. Contributing more than any other fact to strengthen the conviction among the German government classes and in Iperialist circles that Germany could never satisfy her imperialist aspirations without the conquest of colonies, it was this which established in the Imperialist German mind the determination, at any cost, not to let the last *res nullius* remaining, i. e. Turkey, which was really exceptionally important, escape from German influence...... It therefore became more imperative than ever that Austria should maintain her hegemony in the Balkans, for the

sake of German designs, and ultimately of acquiring
Salonika.''*

From our point of view the history of Morocco begins with the Anglo-French treaty of April 8, 1904.
This treaty consisted of two parts, one public and
one secret. The secret part first appeared in French
newspapers late in 1911, after the Morocco crisis of
that year was past.

The public Treaty contains a French acknowledgment of our position in Egypt, and an English acknowledgment, as regards Morocco, ''that it apper-
tains to France, more particularly as a Power whose
dominions are coterminous for a great distance with
those of Morocco, to preserve order in that country,
and to provide assistance for the purpose of all administrative, economic, financial and military reforms
which it may require.'' The two governments agree
not to permit the erection of fortifications on the Moorish coast anywhere near the Straits of Gibraltar, and
France agrees to come to an understanding with Spain
in regard to this portion of the coast. England and
France reciprocally promise each other diplomatic
support in carrying out the agreement, and declare
that they have no intention of altering the political
status of Egypt or Morocco.

The secret articles are concerned with what is to
happen if, nevertheless, England or France should
decide to alter the political status of Egypt or

*The history of Morocco has been so well told by Mr. Morel
(Morocco in Diplomacy'', Smith, Elder & Co., 1912, reprinted
as "Ten Years of Secret Diplomacy, An Unheeded Warning",
1915) that any new account not designed simply to whitewash
the English and French Governments can only repeat what is to
be found in this book, even when, like what follows, it is derived
from other sources.

Morocco.   The article assigning the share of Spain
is as follows:

"The two Governments agree that a certain extent of Morrish territory adjacent to Melilla, Ceuta,
and other présidés should, whenever the Sultan ceases
to exercise authority over it, come within the sphere
of influence of Spain, and that the administration
of the coast from Melilla as far as, but not including, the heights on the right bank of the Sebou shall
be entrusted to Spain.

"Nevertheless, Spain would previously have to give
her formal assent to the provisions of Articles IV
and VII of the Declaration of today's date, and undertake to carry them out.*

"She would also have to undertake not to alienate
the whole, or a part, of the territories placed under
her authority or in her sphere of influence."

Thus the manner in which Morocco was to be par-
titioned between France and Spain was already provided for, in such a way as to allay our fear of seeing
any strong naval Power established in the neighbourhood of the Straits of Gibraltar.   The Treaty contemplated the complete absorption of Morocco by France,
except along the Mediterranean coast, where our naval
interests had to be safeguarded.

When the Entente with France was concluded,
there was almost universal rejoicing in England.
Liberal-minded people were glad to co-operate with
the great leader of continental democracy and liberalism; the friends of peace were glad that all causes

---

*These concern the Open Door, and the absence of fortifica-
tions near Gibraltar.

of friction had been removed between two great nations which had always respected each other; but, strange to say, the Jingoes and Imperialists were also delighted, and the Entente was concluded by the same Government which had made the South African War. This should have made radicals and pacifists think, but it did not. Sir E. Grey, in blessing the Entente, said "it seemed as if some benign influence were at work," bringing friendship instead of enmity into the relations of England and France. Looking back now, we can see what the benign influence was; it was the German Navy. This was the decisive factor that led us to swing over on to the side of the Franco-Russian Alliance. It was not love of French liberalism, nor even of Russian police methods, that produced the Entente: it was fear of Germany. "Our future is on the sea," said the Kaiser, and interpreted this as meaning: "Our future is over England's grave."

Now I do not say that our fear was irrational or groundless, and I do not say that we were wrong to take precautions. What I do say is that the measures which we actually took were ideally calculated to bring the danger nearer, to increase the aggressive temper which was beginning to grow up in Germany, to persuade Germans that we would yield nothing whatever to the claims of justice. I say that the measures we adopted were dictated by panic, and lacked the wisdom, the cool courage, which a calmer survey would have inspired. I say that the ends pursued by our foreign policy were exactly similar to the ends pursued by the German foreign policy, and were pursued by methods which made us accomplices in abominable crimes against humanity and freedom. I say that our policy revived warlike feeling in France, and fostered it in Germany. I say that in 1911 our readiness to provoke a European war was greater than that of Germany, and that our reluctance in 1914 cannot therefore be wholly attributed to disinterested virtue. All this, I think, can be proved by an impartial recital of facts. In this recital, the first and most important chapter is Morocco.

The foreign secretary in France at the time of the conclusion of the Entente was the same as at the time of Fashoda, and the same as the foreign secretary now, M. Delcassé. Before the negotiation of the Entente, M. Delcassé, in pursuit of the policy of colonial expansion, was vehemently anti-English. Since the conclusion of the Entente, he has been vehemently anti-German, because the policy of the *Revanche* has again seemed feasible. Ever since the conclusion of the war of 1870, the fundamental desire of nationalist feeling in France has been for revenge on Germany and the recovery of Alsace-Lorraine. But for long years this policy has seemed so hopeless of success that French ambitions were turned in other directions, and especially towards the acquisition of colonies. This policy produced friction with England, and as an anti-English policy it came to grief at Fashoda. The Entente produced a new possibility; the combination of colonial expansion with the policy of the *Revanche*, both in co-operation with England. Anti-German feeling, which despair had made silent and subterranean, came again to the surface with the revival of hope, and found its protagonist in M. Delcassé.

This policy was not that of Liberal elements in France; it was that of the re-actionaries, the Clericals, the Militarists, and certain financial interests. Liberal opinion in France, seeing that colonial adventures and war-scares were the enemies of social reform, was anxious to abandon hostility to Germany and to be conciliatory as regards Morocco. This party, which had the majority of French Parliament, was feared by our Foreign Office and by "The Times," which allied themselves with all that was least liberal and least pacific in French opinion. If we had genuinely desired peace in Europe, we should have rejoiced in any sign of better relations between France and Germany. In fact, however, we did what we could to make the French nation suspicious of those Frenchmen who tried to be conciliatory in their dealings with Germany, and to suggest that we regarded the progressive elements in French public life as lacking in loyalty to the Entente.

M. Delcassé failed to notify the Morocco Treaty formally to the German Government, presumably in order to show his indifference to German opinion. At the moment, however, Germany showed no resentment.

M. Delcassé next negotiated a secret treaty and a public declaration with Spain, concluded on October 3rd, 1904. The public declaration states that France and Spain "remain firmly attached to the integrity of the Moorish Empire under the Sovereignty of the Sultan." The secret treaty delimits the respective spheres of France and Spain in Morocco, and arranges what is to happen "in case the continuance of the political status of Morocco and of the Shereefian Government should become impossible." The secret treaty first became known to the world through its publication by "Le Matin" in Nov. 1911. Not even the public declaration was officially notified by France to the German Government.

To those who are unaccustomed to diplomatic methods, there is something repellent in the contradictory character of the public declarations and secret understandings of England, France and Spain in the matter of Morocco. Publicly, they stated that they "remained firmly attached" to the integrity of Morocco. Secretly, they arranged how the booty was to be divided in case this attachment should become less firm. If two men were to proclaim publicly that they had no intention of stealing their neighbour's goods, and were at the same time to draw up and sign a careful secret contract as to how his goods were to be shared in case they came into possession of them, they would not be believed if they declared, on being caught, that at the time they sincerely hoped they would remain honest. France and Spain had no right to Morocco except that of contiguity—the very same right which the King had to Naboth's Vineyard. The Moorish Empire was independent, and its international status was regulated by the Madrid Convention of 1880.* If misgovernment were to produce a genuine need for European intervention, the obviously right course was to make the intervention

---

*Which provided (*inter alia*) that all the signatories (among whom Germany was included) should enjoy most-favoured-nation treatment in Morocco.

international, as in the case of the Boxers in China. But this was not the course adopted by England, France and Spain. While publicly declaring that they hoped the integrity of Morocco could be preserved, they secretly arranged who was to have what in case Moroccan independence came to an end. And this contingency was considered sufficiently probable for France to be willing, on account of it, to withdraw its long-standing, opposition to our occupation of Egypt. The analogy is exact with our illustration of the two burglars with the addition of a third who is paid to stand out of the job at the very moment when the two are publicly protesting their wish to remain honest.

Professor Murray has a charmingly idyllic explanation of the secrecy which was preserved as to the terms of partition. No diplomat, I feel sure, could have thought of anything so idyllic—which shows the wisdom of summoning outside assistance for the defence of the Foreign Office. Professor Murray's explanation is, that the political status of Morocco would have been more difficult to maintain if it had become known that England and France contemplated the possibility of having to change it; and so anxious were the two Powers to do nothing to hasten the downfall of Morocco, that, like benevolent bedside doctors, they concealed the danger from the patient and from his friends. This was very kind, certainly. But the kindness did not end here. One of the doctors, who had expectations from the patient's demise, paid the other to leave him in sole charge, and subsequently administered many small

doses of poison. Finally, the patient died, and the
doctor came into his inheritance. Those who can believe, with Professor Murray, that he grieved sincerely for the sick man's death, are to be congratulated on their charitable disposition.

Germany, at first, raised no objections to the Anglo-
French treaty or to the Franco-Spanish declaration.
France proceeded to urge upon the Moorish Govern-
ment a series of reforms which even Professor
Murray regards as "perhaps too much concerned with
French interest and monopolies." What ensued may
be told in Professor Murray's words:

"The Shereef procrastinated, the pressure continued, when suddenly, on March 31st, 1905, the German Emperor in person descended in his private
yacht on the port of Tangier, and made a speech to
the world at large. He announced that he regarded
the Shereef as a free and independent sovereign, not
bound to obey any foreign pressure; that sudden and
sweeping reforms were undesirable in Morocco; and
that German interests must be safeguarded.

This speech was followed by a demand for a general European conference to settle the affairs of
Morocco."

What are we to think of this characteristically
dramatic action? In manner it was brutal, in substance it showed more concern for German national
interests than for friendly relations between the
Great Powers. In both these respects it was to be
condemned. There can be little doubt that it was
encouraged by the weakness of Russia owing to the
Manchurian defeats. But it should also be said that

the existence of a secret Franco-Spanish treaty was known, and it is not improbable that its terms, as well as the secret articles of the Anglo-French treaty, had been discovered by the German secret service. However that may be, the Kaiser's action was indefensible, on the broad ground that it was calculated to provoke resentment in England and France.

But I think we must give a different answer when we ask whether this resentment, however natural, was justified by the facts. The Kaiser's discourtesy was only a retort to the deliberate discourtesy of M. Delcassé in not notifying the German Government of the treaty of April and the declaration of October. The exclusive nationalism of the Kaiser's attitude was merely the parallel to the exclusive nationalism of England and France in attempting to dispose of Morocco as suited themselves, without considering the natural resentment likely to be felt in Germany. As regards the substance of the dispute, Germany's legal case was good and ours was bad. Let us take the points mentioned by Professor Murray. The Kaiser "announced that he regarded the Shereef as a free and independent sovereign"—Franch and Britain had made practically the same announcement in their public treaty. The Shereef could only cease to be free and independent owing to the military conquest of his dominions, or the financial strangulation which sometimes secures the same end more cheaply. The Kaiser had as good a right to declare him free and independent as we have to declare King Albert free and independent, and we had as little legal right to decree the subjection of Morocco

as the Kaiser has to decree the subjection of Belgium.
I admit that it was unplausible to maintain, "that
sudden and sweeping reforms were undesirable in
Morocco," at any rate, if it was so, Morocco must
have differed from every other part of the earth's
surface. But the men who wanted to reform Morocco
were resisting reforms at home, and were demanding
reform in their own interest, rather than in that of
Morocco. So much is implied in Professor Murray's
allusion to "French interests and monopolies." The
assertion that "German interests must be safeguarded," though not one with which I sympathise,
is one which is considered the duty of every Government, and for which Professor Murray praises Mr.
Lloyd George's Mansion House speech in 1911. The
Madrid Convention of 1880 guaranteed to Germany,
along with other Powers, most-favoured-nation treatment in Morocco, and Germany's right to safeguard
this position was indisputable. Finally, we came to
the Kaiser's demand for an international Conference
to decide the status of Morocco. This demand was
so unquestionably just that Professor Murray can
find nothing to say against it. "The future of
Morocco," he confesses, "was a matter of public interest, and the rest of Europe had the right to be
consulted." And again: "France's case was not
perfect; if we had been absolutely disinterested arbi-
trators in the matter, we should probably have decided that France ought to agree to a conference."
He remarks, in his amiable way, that "the end, as it
happened, seemed exactly to satisfy the demands of
justice." But the demands of justice were not satis-

fied until Germany had threatened war, until England had shown a complete willingness to fight in a quarrel in which Professor Murray admits that we were in the wrong, and M. Delcassé, in spite of our hot support, had been dismissed from office by the good sense of the French nation, not, as "The Times" has taught Englishmen to believe, at the insolent bidding of the Kaiser.

Professor Murray deals with our initial opposition to a conference in the following terms:

"France, to whom we had promised our diplomatic support, seemed, in her indignation at being bullied, to be inclined to refuse a conference. And we took our stand firmly at her side.

"It would be interesting to know what our representatives said in private to our friends' representatives. It is likely enough that there were private warnings and appeals for moderation. But in public, at any rate, Great Britain stood with perfect loyalty by the side of France. Here, no doubt, we strike upon one of Sir E. Grey's cardinal principles: if you make an engagement, carry out your engagement loyally and with no hedging."

It is a comfort to know that Sir E. Grey possesses this virtue; perhaps Professor Murray is also able to assure us that the Chancellor of the Exchequer does not embezzle public funds and the Home Secretary does not levy blackmail on burglars in return for immunity from arrest. I am sorry Professor Murray should have allowed himself to imply that Sir E. Grey is exceptional among British Foreign Secretaries in the practice of keeping his promises,

the more so as he was not Foreign Secretary at the
time that Professor Murray is dealing with. The
Kaiser's visit to Tangier, and the opposition of England and France to a conference, occurred while Lord
Lansdowne was still at the Foreign Office.

What Professor Murray says about loyalty to en-
gagements and the likelihood of "private warnings
and appeals for moderation" is exactly what, if he
were a German, he would say about Germany's attitude to Austria during the twelve days. The cases
are exactly similar; we do not know what was said,
but such evidence as we possess tends to show that
Germany egged on Austria and England egged on
France. The evidence in each case is inconclusive,
but it is considerably stronger in the case of England and France in 1905* than in the case of Germany and Austria in 1914. War did not result at
the earlier date, because French public opinion saw
the madness of M. Delcassé's policy; war was averted
by democratic control. In Austria, with its monarch-
ical constitution, this restraining force was absent.

It is not very easy to draw conclusions as to the
extent of our support of France in 1905 from the
mass of contradictory evidence, of which I have
given an account in the Appendix B. In view of the
line which we know to have been taken later by Sir
E. Grey, the most probable hypothesis would seem
to be that Lord Lansdowne, while refusing to make a
promise, consented to make a prophecy, and to state
that, in his opinion, Parliament would support the
Government if the occasion for giving armed assist-

---

*See Appendix B.

ance to France should rise. From the point of view of honour, such a prophecy has very nearly the same binding force as a promise. Any action which the French might have taken on the strength of it would obviously have compelled our Government to exert all its influence at home in order to secure the realisation of its prophecy, and if our Government had failed, no one could deny that the French would have had a legitimate grievance against us.

Whether or not our action in 1905 was as I have supposed, it certainly was of this nature in the later crisis of 1911, when the French case was scarcely better than in 1905. But before we come to the crisis of 1911, we must say a few words about the Conference of Algeciras and the subsequent actions of the French at Morocco.

The privileges secured by the French under the Act of Algeciras were very few; it is misleading to say, as Professor Murray does, that the delegates "decided almost all points in favour of France and against Germany." The sum-total of the concessions secured by France, Spain and England were the three following:

(1) There was to be a force of native police, numbering between two thousand and two thousand five hundred, which was to be under Spanish and French inspectors numbering sixteen to twenty officers, and thirty to forty non-commissioned officers— the whole being subject to an Inspector General, who was to be a superior officer of the Swiss Army.

(2) A Morocco State Bank was to be established as the financial agent of the Moorish Government;

this Bank was to be subject to French law, to have its
capital subscribed in equal shares by the signatories
of the Algeciras Act, and to have, in addition to the
Board of Directors, and to a High Commissioner
appointed by the Moroccan Government after consul-
tation with the directors, four Censors, appointed respectively by the German Imperial Bank, the Bank of
England, the Bank of Spain, and the Bank of France.
The Censors were to see that the intentions of the
Act were duly executed, but must "not at any time,
or under any pretext whatsoever, be allowed to interfere in the conduct of the business or in the internal administration of the Bank." The annual
Report of the Censors was to be unanimous.

(3)  On the Algerian frontier, and in the Riff
country, the carrying out of the regulations made by
the Act as regards customs and the trade in arms and
explosives should not be in the hands of an international authority, but in the hands of France and
Morocco in the former region and Spain and Morocco
in the latter.

Thus France and Spain acquired a right to not more
than sixty inspectors of police under the command of
a Swiss; to a majority of three to one (counting England as on their side) among the Censors, whose
powers, however, seem to have depended upon
unanimity, and to exclusive co-operation with the
Moors in carrying out certain provisions of the Act
on the borders of their own territories.

The last Article (No. CXXIII) of the Act is as
follows:

"All existing Treaties, Conventions, and Arrangements between the Signatory Powers and Morocco remain in force. It is, however, agreed that, in case their provisions be found to conflict with those of the present General Act, the stipulations of the latter shall prevail.''

It is clear that the Act gave to every signatory Power the legal right to give or withhold its consent before any action was taken which contravened the Act. This gave Germany its *locus standi* in subsequent disputes. The formal correctness of Germany's position in the following years is thus indisputable, whatever we may think of the manner in which the Kaiser chose to press his claims.

If the Moors had been capable of preserving order, the Act of Algeciras might have proved an insuperable barrier to French ambitions. It may be that, as Professor Murray maintains, order could not have been preserved by the Moorish authorities even if no European had been at hand to profit by disturbances. However that may be, it is clear that the usual methods of proving the incompetence of a semi-civilised Government were adopted. As Professor Murray observes: ''French intrigues, German intrigues, Spanish intrigues, intrigues of financiers and speculators free from any particular national bias: All these causes are freely alleged to have been in operation, and it would need a bold man to meet such charges with a denial.''

In any case France (and to a less degree Spain) profited by every failure of the Moors, and occupied one portion after another of Moroccan territory. In February, 1909, in a Franco-German declaration, the

Germans acknowledged that France had special interests in Morocco, while the French promised not to obstruct German economic interests in that country, and declared, as usual, their firm attachment to its independence and integrity. But this declaration proved only a halting-place, not a definite solution.

In April, 1911, owing to the supposed danger to Europeans in Fez from neighbouring tribes in revolt, the French sent an expedition which occupied the town, and was followed by a larger force which succeeded in putting down the rebellion. Frenchmen who were opposed to a forward policy in Morocco maintained, with much force or argument, that there never was any danger to Europeans in Fez. Those of us who remember the terrible accounts of (wholly imaginary) dangers to women and children in Johannesburg before the Jameson Raid will be slow to decide that the danger in Fez must have been real. I have no means of ascertaining the truth, and Professor Murray also has apparently been unable to find evidence of danger, for he says:

"The Radical opposition in France maintain, rightly and wrongly, that the Europeans in Fez were in no real danger and that the expedition was unnecessary; but that difficult question does not come within our present purview."

We may gather from this admission that, whether there was danger or not, our Foreign Office, at least, possesses no evidence of its existence. When the French expedition started, the French Government announced that it would withdraw after succouring the Europeans. But the pressure of the French

Colonial Party proved too strong, and the troops remained in occupation of the capital. The Germans, from the first, adopted an attitude which was perfectly within their rights. They raised no objection to the relief of Fez, but they pointed out that, if the occupation continued, it could no longer be maintained that Morocco was still independent. In these circumstances, since the Act of Algeciras was to be modified, the Germans demanded compensation for their consent. France was obtaining an advantage which had been refused by the Act of Algeciras, and, since the old German policy of upholding Moroccan independence had become impossible, Germany was willing to part with its rights in Morocco for a price. This is exactly the attitude which would be adopted in private life by a business man in a similar situation. It is not a noble attitude, not an attitude compatible with a keen desire for international amity; but it is an attitude involving only that degree of national self-seeking which is, unfortunately, taken for granted in the foreign policy of all Great Powers. It is no better, but also no worse, than the policy of other countries in similar circumstances.

Professor Murray's comment on Germany's action is as follows:

"If there was plunder going she insisted that she should have her share. Such a claim was not particularly creditable nor strictly just. But, in the atmosphere of colonial policy, it was intelligible."

With this account, in the main, I have no fault to find. I agree with the statement that the German claim was "not particularly creditable." It would

have been far more creditable to say: "France, perhaps unavoidably, has broken the Act of Algeciras,
and, if I stood on the letter of my rights, I might
demand compensation.  But goodwill between the
nations is more important than the acquisition of
colonies by Germany, and I will waive my rights in
order to show that I wish to live at peace with all
the world."  This is what an enlightened and humane
Government would have said, and this is not what the
German Government said.  But the English and
French Governments, equally, were not inspired by
enlightened and human ideas; if they had been, the
crisis would never have arisen.

To say that the German Government's demand was
"not strictly just," seems to me to be going too far.
Justice was the one merit which it might claim.
France, rightly or wrongly, was acting contrary to
the Act of Algeciras, and Germany had a clear legal
right to expect payment for acquiescence.  Germany's
formal case, as in 1905, was good.  As in that case,
what was wrong with Germany was brutality in
method and indifference to international good will.

France, with the support of England, showed an
equal indifference to international good will, and
England showed an almost equal brutality of method.
Moreover, the French case was technically bad,
whereas the German case was technically good.  In
view of the Act of Algeciras, the French ought, from
the first, to have professed a willingness to seek the
consent of the Powers before effecting any alteration
in the status of Morocco.  Assuming that the expedition to Fez was justified by danger to Europeans, the

French ought, at the moment of dispatching it, to
have declared that, since the independence of Morocco
had become impossible, they were willing to submit
the decision as to its future to a new conference. Both
legally, and from the broad point of view of humanity and friendship between States, this is what France
ought to have done, and what we ought to have ad-
vised France to do.

This, however, is not what France did, or what we,
apparently, wished France to do. France, says
Professor Murray, "saw no good reason why she
should make sacrifices. The demands for compensation, whatever they were, were not accepted; the
French Government showed unwillingness to come to
a private understanding with Germany." France
"saw no good reason!" The good reason was, first,
that Germany's demand was legally justifiable; secondly, that to refuse it obviously involved risk of a
European war, with all its devastation, for the sake
of an essentially petty question of territory in equa-
torial Africa.* Thirdly, that by not giving way at
once it would be made apparent to Germany that bare
justice could not be obtained from the Triple Entente
except by force or the threat of force; fourthly, that
the French action accentuated the division of Europe
into two camps, and was ideally calculated to increase
the growing militarism and aggressiveness of the Germans. All this Professor Murray passes by in silence;
all this, which subsequent history has bitterly confirmed, he regards as too unimportant to mention.

---

*Territory in Morocco was never in question. See below.

In the Agadir crisis** the methods and purposes
of England and Germany were exactly similar; the
despatch of the *Panther* was provocative and brutal,
and so was Mr. Lloyd George's Mansion House speech.
The chief difference is that, in 1911, we were willing
to fight and the Germans were not. The main facts
are not in dispute, and are quite enough to establish
the reckless folly of our policy at that time.

After France had shown unwillingness to come to a
private understanding with Germany on the question
of compensation elsewhere for the recognition of the
French protectorate in Morocco, the German Government sent a gunboat, the *Panther,* followed by a
cruiser, the *Berlin,* to the harbour of Agadir on the
south coast of Morocco. (July 1, 1911). This action
was provocative and tactless; the only thing to be
said in extenuation is that it was only taken after
the French had shown themselves unwilling to yield
to the claims of mere justice. It was intended to
show that Germany was in earnest, and to produce
a more yielding spirit on the part of France in the
matter of compensation. What troubled our Foreign
Office, however,* was not the fear of war between
France and Germany, but, on the contrary, the fear
that they might reach an agreement which would be

---

**Professor Murray has performed a service to the critics of
diplomacy and its methods by his account of the Agadir crisis.
Most Englishmen who have not made a study of foreign policy
find it difficult to believe that our Government can have done
things which in fact it did do. The evidence is mostly contained
in old newspapers, Land Blue Books, and is therefore somewhat
inaccessible. But Professor Murray's statement of the facts is
quite sufficient to establish the case against our Foreign Office,
and includes everything that is stated without special authority
in what follows. While intending to praise England and decry
Germany, he involuntarily makes it plain that the facts totally
fail to establish his client's innocence.

prejudicial to our interests. We feared, or professed
to fear, that the Germans might acquire a naval base
on the Atlantic, and that our trade interests might
be injuriously affected. Neither France nor Germany
in the period from July 1 to Mr. Lloyd George's Mansion House Speech (July 21), kept us adequately informed of the course of the negotations, although Sir
E. Grey, on July 4, informed the German Ambassador
that we could not be disinterested in the matter of
Morocco. We were afraid that the bargain was going
to be conducted without our participation, and this,
it was felt, could not be borne.

Several reasons have been given why we had to
intervene.* Let us examine them.

(1) "We had our own definite interests in
Morocco; our Moroccan trade, and the strategical importance of the north coast."

As regards our strategical interests, it is enough
to point out that Germany made it clear from the
first that what was sought as compensation was not
a portion of Morocco, ** but a portion (or, some said,
the whole) of the French Congo, where our strategical
interests were too minute to deserve serious consideration. And so far as trade is concerned, our interest

---

*The reasons examined are those given by Professor Murray.
They are the same as those given by other apologists. The
quotations are from him.
**M. de Selves (the French Foreign Minister), stated in the
Debate of Dec. 14, 1911, that, in reply to the French claim to
Morocco, Germany replied: "Right, we accept. Take Morocco,
establish your Protectorate there. But since you have made
a treaty with England in this matter, since you have made a
treaty with Italy, since you have made a treaty with Spain, on
what basis will you treat with us? Our public opinion does not
permit that we should not obtain elsewhere some compensation
for our abandonment in your favour and the promise which we
shall give you that our diplomacy will assist in getting the
Powers to ratify the arrangement we arrive at." (Quoted by
Morel, p. 177).

is exactly the same as Germany's in any territory controlled by France, namely, the preservation of the Open Door. We had secured this for thirty years in 1904, the Germans secured it permanently in 1911. It should have been obvious to our diplomatists that any change demanded by the Germans as regards trade must be to our advantage. This first reason thus falls to the ground.

(2) It is argued that we had to guard against two opposite dangers; Germany might force war on France, or might make friends with France and detach her from Great Britain. The first of these alternatives seems to have troubled us very little; for if France felt a wish for our help, France could appeal for it, and make us a party to the negotiations. What troubled us was, that we were not a party to the negotiations; and in this France need not have concurred except by her own choice. It is perfectly clear throughout the crisis that what we feared was not a rupture, but an agreement prejudicial to our interests, and it seems that "The Times," at least, would have regarded as prejudicial to our interests any agreement which produced genuinely friendly relations between France and Germany.* This is also the view of Professor Murray. He says:

"Germany might try the policy of detaching France from Great Britain. We had ourselves had the experience of her attempt to detach us from France. (See below, pp 115ff.) She might now be trying to persuade France privately to promise neutrality in Germany's next war, as she tried in the previous

---

*See "Times" of July 20, despatch from Paris.

year to persuade us. There was naturally a party in France which was somewhat shy of commitments to Great Britain, and might be glad to obtain temporary security at the price of dissolving the Entente. This danger would become greater if Great Britain took no step to show that she would stand by France in the present difficulty. So from this point of view, also, we are bound to show our interest in France.''

This paragraph is truly astonishing. On referring to p. 115, to see what Macchiavellian plot Germany had attempted to entice us into, we find the following, in the account of the Anglo-German negotiations of 1909: ''The Chancellor's general proposal of co-operation centred in an engagement that, in the event of either Power being attacked by a third Power or group of Powers, the Power attacked should remain neutral.'' That is to say, the dark design of Germany, which put us on our guard during the Agadir crisis, was a design to induce us to promise not to take part in an aggressive war against Germany. We refused, according to Professor Murray, to give any such undertaking. And if we had given it, he says: ''The confidence between France and Great Britain would have been sapped.''

Of course, he goes on to say that we had no aggressive intentions. At the same time, Germany knew that we had been willing to fight in 1905, when France had a bad case and gave way; Germany was to find us still willing to fight in 1911, when France still had a bad case. Is it surprising if Germany, remembering that we had lately refused to promise neutrality if Germany were attacked, seeing that we

were obviously afraid of friendly relations between
France and Germany, and not afraid to threaten war,
came to the conclusion that we desired a trial of
strength between Germany and the Entente? As
regards the immense majority of Englishmen, this
was the absolute opposite of the truth. But the Foreign Office and "The Times" had so conducted our
affairs that the Germans could not well come to any
other conclusion. And it is only just to remember
this fact when we condemn them—as we are right in
doing—for their bellicose attitude in the summer of
1914.*

"There was naturally," we are told, "a party in
France which is somewhat shy of commitments to
Great Britain." There was indeed such a party,
just as there was in England—a party which contained almost all the Radical and Labour elements,
and all who regarded the preservation of peace as the
most important aim of foreign policy. The party in
France which desired commitments to Great Britain,
like the party in Great Britain which desired commitments to France, consisted of the militarists, imperialists, and reactionaries. In France, as in England,
it was this party which controlled the acts of the
Government, while the Radical party as a rule controlled its speeches. While the militarists saw with
rejoicing the tendency of the acts of the two Govern-

---

*It is in the light of Professor Murray's references to p. 115
of his pamphlet that we must interpret his statement that
Germany "might now (in July, 1911), be trying to persuade
France privately to promise neutrality in Germany's next war,
*as she tried in the previous year to persuade us*" (my italics).
That is to say, Germany might be trying to persuade France
to promise neutrality if Germany were attacked. It is this
danger, apparently, which Professor Murray regards as justifying
our provocative attitude in the Agadir crisis.

ments, the Radicals in both countries, unsuspicious, anxious for promised reforms at home, and mostly unversed in the details of diplomacy, were placated by soft words, and by assurances, misleading even if verbally accurate, that no obligation of support in war existed on either side.

And so, in spite of the legal rectitude of Germany's claim, we stood by France, according to the Foreign Office apologist, in the hope of securing French support on some future occasion when we might be advancing some equally unjust claim. Truly an astonishing defence!

(3) Finally we come to the supreme reason for our intervention: the fetich of "prestige." What we are told is this:

"Hardly less imperative was the mere matter of prestige. We had been for many years the chief commercial Power in Morocco; we had vital interests in the north coast. We had taken a leading part in the various treaties. We could hardly submit to the indignity of being suddenly treated as non-existent, while Germany settled with France, in a manner which she refused to explain to us, the future of Morocco."

I am glad Professor Murray has written this paragraph. If I had written it, it would have been considered a gross libel upon those who direct our policy, and it would have caused my printer and publisher to be sent to prison under the Defence of the Realm Act. But as Professor Murray has written it, we have it on unimpeachable authority that our prestige in the matter of Morocco was considered one of the grave and weighty reasons on account of which our Government told Mr. Lloyd George to speak as he did at the Mansion House, and behaved throughout the crisis in a way that must embitter our relations with Germany, and must have led to war if France and Germany had not both been more reasonable than England.

There is a homely proverb that "sauce for the goose is sauce for the gander." It appears that Professor Murray does not believe this proverb, for, when discussing M. Delcassé's failure to notify the treaty of 1904 to the German Government, he says that M. Delcassé

"Objected strongly to the idea that France must submit her important acts of foreign policy to Germany for approval, except in matters where Germany was directly concerned. Here he was doubtless right; the claim which Germany afterwards made, that no treaty should be made in any part of the world without the approval of Germany, was not one which a self-respecting nation could admit."

Yet this claim, which "no self-respecting nation could admit," was precisely analogous to the claim of prestige which we advanced in 1911, when we decided that "we could hardly submit to the dignity of being suddenly treated as non-existent." True, he had treaty obligations towards the French in Morocco, but what were they? To leave the French a free hand, and to give them diplomatic support when they wanted it. Our intervention in 1911 amounted to refusing them a free hand, and intervening on the side of one party in their political disputes. This was not demanded of us by the treaty of 1904, and if it had been, the French would never have consented to conclude such a treaty. Our claim of prestige had nothing to do with treaty obligations; it was a claim of national pride, exactly analogous to the German claim which we are all agreed in regarding as preposterous.

What was this "prestige" which we felt to be endangered by the negotiations between France and Germany? Apart from prestige, our trade interests and our strategical interests were not endangered, since Germany claimed no territory in Morocco, and desired the Open Door, which was what our trade required. One vital interest we had, if our policy was to continue on the lines pursued since 1904: it was essential to our policy that France and Germany should remain on bad terms with each other. This purpose, which we could not avow, was achieved by Mr. Lloyd George's Mansion House speech; but this was not a matter of mere prestige. Prestige is nothing but standing on one's dignity—that foolish kind of "dignity" which is affected by people who feel their position insecure and are always looking out for insults. Mr. A., hearing that his friend Mr. B. is giving a dinner party to which he has invited his rival Mr. C., sends word to Mr. C. that unless Mr. B. is induced to invite him also, Mr. C. shall be starved, his outlying fields devastated, and anyone who attempts to defend them killed. Mr. C. replies that Mr. B. has a right to invite or not invite anyone he pleases, but if he yields to Mr. A.'s pressure, his house shall be burned down, his labourers put to

death, and himself reduced to beggary. Mr. A. re-
torts that Mr. C. is a brute; Mr. C. rejoins that Mr.
A. is an insolent busybody. Meanwhile Mr. B., with
infinite trouble, smooths the ruffled dignity of his
angry neighbours, who have made him the pawn in
their rivalry. Strange to say, he is expected to feel
gratitude to Mr. A. for the dangers to which Mr.
A. has exposed him. This is the Agadir crisis in a
parable—except that Germany's attitude was more
reasonable than that of Mr. C.

It is not plain to every man possessed of either
humanity or common sense that this whole game of
prestige is childish and brutal? The only true interest of England, the only true interest of mankind,
in the Agadir dispute, was that it should be settled in the manner least likely to lead to war or to
leave a legacy of international ill-will. The Germans
chose to press their rights to the utmost. In doing
so, they were acting the part of the insecure *parvenu*
saying: "I am a Great Power too; don't you forget it!" But the conduct of England, instead of
being such as to allay this mood, was such as to in-
flame it. England's position as a Great Power, one
would have thought, was sufficiently secure to be able
to endure an outward yielding to the claims of a
Power whose dignity is more recent and more un-
easy. We ought to have met Germany's desire for
school-boy triumphs with the tolerant smile of an
elder brother. Instead of doing so, we refused to
acknowledge the badness of our case, and reduced our
manners to the German level by putting up Mr. Lloyd
George to administer a scolding.

We had desired from the first to be a party to the Franco-German negotiations, and on July 4, Sir E. Grey informed the German Ambassador that we could not recognise any arrangements that might be come to without us. As nothing came of this, Sir E. Grey made a more emphatic statement to the German Ambassador on July 21, and on the very same evening Mr. Lloyd George spoke at the Mansion House. After the usual praise of peace, he proceeded as follows:

"But I am also bound to say this—that I believe it is essential in the highest interests, not merely of this country but of the world, that Britain should at all hazards maintain her place and her prestige amongst the Great Powers of the world. Her potent influence has many a time been in the past, and may yet be in the future, invaluable to the cause of human liberty. It has more than once in the past redeemed Continental nations, who are sometimes too apt to forget that service, from overwhelming disaster and even from international extinction. I would make great sacrifices to preserve peace. I conceive that nothing would justify a disturbance of international good will except questions of the gravest national moment. But if a situation were to be forced upon us in which peace could only be preserved by the surrender of the great and beneficent position Great Britain has won by centuries of heroism and achievement, by allowing Britain to be treated where her interests were vitally affected as if she were of no account in the Cabinet of Nations, then I say emphatically that peace at that price would be a humiliation intolerable for a great country like ours to endure.''

The meaning of this speech could not be doubtful. It was a public threat to Germany, a clear intimation that we were prepared to go to war in defence of our interests in the Moroccan question. What those interests were, we have seen: Treaty obligations towards France, which were not in question and were not invoked by the French; prestige, which no rational man can regard as anything but folly; and lastly, as the unavowed motive of the whole policy, a fear of good relations between France and Germany, lest France should fail us when the day came for a trial of strength between us and the Germans. That the German Government looked forward to such a day, I am not prepared to deny. But a plain narrative of events makes it evident that we were, at that time, even more willing to hasten the day than the Germans were. The clash between the Entente and the Central Empires was brought about by a series of steps, some great and some small. Some of these steps were taken by one side, some by the other. One of the longest steps towards war was taken by the British Government's action during the Agadir crisis, culminating in Mr. Lloyd George's diatribe at the Mansion House. For this reason, among others, the British Government cannot escape its share of responsibility for the final catastrophe.

For a few days after the 21st, relations between England and Germany were strained almost to breaking point. But the forces in Germany on the side of peace—apparently supported, at that time, by the Kaiser—exerted all their strength, and an agreement was arrived at. We became a party to the negotiations, the German claims were found not to conflict with our interests, and on November 4, Conventions were concluded between France and Germany recognising the French protectorate in Morocco in return for a cession of territory in the French Congo. So far as diplomacy was concerned, these Conventions constituted the final solution of the Moroccan question. The solution itself was not objectionable, and was such as might have been reached without difficulty by sensible men genuinely desirous of coming to an agreement.

But although the diplomatic question was settled, the bad effects on public opinion remained. The English, who believed Mr. Lloyd George to be a genuine lover of peace, were persuaded that he must have had grave secret reasons for his outburst; the *Panther* at Agadir reminded them of the Kaiser's speech at Tangier in 1905, and they became convinced that German policy was wantonly aggressive, always troubling the international situation, always ready to plunge the world into war; misled by "The Times," the English people remained ignorant of the German case, and unaware that they and the French had been the real aggressors. The French, finding that the English Government was ready to stand by them in a war with Germany, became far more bellicose than they had been; the *revanche* began to seem a possibility, men who had been pacifists became jingoes, the Three Years' Service Law was introduced, and the whole tone of French politics was changed. As for the effect on Germany, it has been related with startling candour in the French Yellow Book.* The Germans—unreasonably, as it seems to us, regarded the agreement which was reached as a humiliation, and decided that they would not again be compelled to submit to threats. The Kaiser—so it is stated—became convinced that war was inevitable before long, and joined the war-party which he had previously held in check. Preparations of every kind were pushed forward, and in 1914, the reasons, whatever they were, which made Germany fear war in 1911, no longer existed. There can be no doubt whatever that Germany's unyielding stiffness in 1914 was largely due to humiliation at having yielded to our threats at the time of the Agadir crisis, just as Russia's uncompromising attitude was caused by memory of humiliation in 1908 in the matter of Bosnia and Herzegovina. Both Germany and Russia had suffered one humiliation, and each felt that another would ruin its prestige. Each stood firm; and the war is the price which all the nations have to pay for the past triumphs of their diplomatists.

---

*See especially Chapter I, No. 5.

## III. THE ANGLO-RUSSIAN ENTENTE

On August 31, 1907, an Agreement was concluded between England and Russia, by which their outstanding differences were settled. In Tibet, both parties agreed to seek no advantages, either in the way of territory or of economic concessions. In Afghanistan, Russia recognized British suzerainty. In Persia, a Russian sphere in the north and a British sphere in the south were marked out, with a neutral zone between: each party recognized the independence and integrity of Persia, but nevertheless each recognized the other's special rights in their respective spheres. The Russian sphere included the capital, Teheran, and stretched as far south as Ispahan. The English sphere included about half of what remained: it gave us control of the Gulf, of the Baluchistan frontier, and of the oil wells which have since been used to supply fuel to our battleships.

In the rather complicated negotiations which preceded the conclusion of the Agreement, both England and Russia showed considerable skill: incidentally, we could not but help the Russian Government in suppressing the Duma, in reconquering Poland, and in depriving the Finns of the liberties which the Tsar had sworn to defend. On both sides, it was seen that, owing to the Franco-Russian Alliance, an understanding between England and Russia was necessary in order to complete the Anglo-French Entente. But certain difficulties stood in the way: on the one hand, our alliance with Japan, on the other hand, the strong tendency of Russian policy to an understanding with Germany.

The original Anglo-Japanese Alliance of 1902 bound England and Japan to come to each other's assistance in case either was attacked by two or more Powers. This treaty made it clear that it would not be to the interest of Russia to invoke the aid of France in the Japanese war of 1904-5, since the aid of France would entail the enmity of England. England and France were thus able to maintain the friendliness resulting from the recent Entente, but England and Russia were on very bad terms throughout the time of the Manchurian Campaign. Public opinion in England would have welcomed war with Russia in 1904, when the Russian fleet fired upon our fishing boats under the impression that they were Japanese Destroyers. But the Cabinet, notably Mr. Balfour, foreseeing the need of an Entente with Russia, calmed public opinion and arrived at a friendly settlement of the dispute. Nevertheless, in August, 1905, at almost the same moment as the conclusion of peace between Russia and Japan, the Anglo-Japanese Treaty was renewed and strengthened, each Power now binding itself to come to the assistance of the other even if only one Power were to attack it. Although this Treaty, like that of 1902, was essentially directed against Russia, it facilitated the conclusion of our Entente with Russia, since it destroyed any hope that Russia might otherwise have had of renewing the Far Eastern adventure under more favourable circumstances.*

The new policy is very clearly expressed in a resolution passed by the Latin-Slav League in Paris at the beginning of October, 1905.** This resolution is as follows:

"As the war of Russia, protector of the Slavonic races, against the Anglo-Japanese Alliance is definitely terminated, the political situation is entirely changed. German expansion constitutes the single danger for peace, as is shown by the Morocco incident. The Slavonic races are continually menaced by Germany and her Turkish satellites. The League has decided to protect Slavonic interests by the propagation of an Anglo-French-Russian Alliance to stop the extermination of the Slavonic races and put an end to the enslaving of white races in Europe during the 20th century."

Meanwhile an influential party in Russia, headed by M. Witte, were in favour of an Agreement with Germany rather than with England. This project was used, both by the Russians and by the English advocates of the Entente with Russia, to make England yield claims and principles which otherwise might have formed an obstacle. Imperialists saw dangers in the Russian designs on Persia. Radicals disliked siding with the bureaucracy against the revolution which broke out in October, 1905. The *Times* St. Petersburg Government Correspondent, on October 2, reports that the Russian Government quite recognizes the desirability of coming to terms with England, but is very much averse to having its

*See e. g. St. Petersburg Correspondent in *The Times*, September 5, 7 and 8, 1905.
***Times, October* 3, 1905.

hand forced, and considers that what happens in
Persia will show best whether England is anxious to
be friends or not. The same Correspondent, meanwhile, explains that the Witte school means to play
off Germany against England (September 25).

"It is no longer a secret," he says on October 24*,
"that Germany has exerted every effort to defeat the
Anglo-Russian Entente, and has held out to the Russian Government the most alluring inducements. The
precise nature of Germany's offers has not yet been
divulged. I am informed, however, that the proposals
had reference to joint action in the Baltic and in the
ultimate apportionment of Austria-Hungary."

The German scheme, he said, found a ready advocate in M. Witte, but emphatic opposition from
France. The Paris Correspondent of *The Times*, on
October 26, at the height of the Russian Revolution,
gives details of Germany's offers to Russia on the occasion of M. Witte's visit to Berlin reported by the
("Petit Parisien".)   Germany, we are assured,
offered military intervention in case of a Polish ris-
ing, and the prospective partition of Austria, according to which Russia was to have Bohemia, the Polish
provinces, and other Slav regions, while Germany
took the German-speaking regions and thus secured
a route to the Adriatic. In addition the Kaiser is said
to have proposed to close the Baltic and to guarantee
the Russian and German ports against attack.

It is not credible that Germany should have really
offered to partition so firm an Ally as Austria-Hungary for the benefit of Russia, which could never be

---

*Times*, October 25

attached to the German interest by any very firm
or reliable bond. The Russian motive in spreading
such reports is obvious: fear of Germany made us
more willing to come to terms with Russia. The motive of *The Times* is less obvious; presumably the object was to weaken the public opinion at home which
looked with suspicion on any approach to alliance with
the Russian bureaucracy.

Meanwhile the Russian Government's need of support, either from Germany of from England and
France, was becoming desperate. The disorders
throughout the country grew worse and worse, until
on October 31 the Tsar was forced to grant a Constitution. The Kaiser's sympathies were of course
against the revolution but in France and England
every generous mind saw the progress of events with
joy: all but a few extreme reactionaries watched with
breathless sympathy the devoted courage of the Russian reformers, and hoped passionately for the end
of the most harmful of all tyrannies that weighed
down the human spirit.

At this point, high politics intervened. One main
reason for the success of the Revolution was the
mutinous condition of the Russian Army and Navy,
which could not be remedied without considerable
expenditure. In the disturbed state of the country,
it was difficult to raise revenue. The partisans of the
Duma, which had been granted nominal control over
taxation, wished to secure its position and to carry
much-needed reforms before relieving the Government of its financial embarrassments. The German
Government, which would gladly have repressed the

Revolution, had no capital to spare from its own needs. France, which had hitherto financed Russia, began to feel both that the security was shaky, and that support of the bureaucracy was unworthy of a Liberal Power. M. Clemenceau, in the (*"Aurore"*), warned the French against any participation in Russian loans while the internal condition of affairs remained unsettled: "After having furnished the Tsar," he wrote, "with the financial resources which were destined to lead to his defeat abroad, it now remains for us supply him with the financial resources destined to assure his victory over his own subjects."*
According to *"Gil Blas"*, the representatives of Parisian finance, during January, 1906, drew up conditions for any fresh loan to Russian, involving the granting of full control over finance to the Duma.**
All Liberal opinion in Russia was against the conclusion of a loan while the powers of the Duma remained in doubt. On April 9, 1906, the *Times* Correspondent at St. Petersburg telegraphed:—***

"The Opposition organs continue their campain against the conclusion of a foreign loan before the Duma meets. A host of arguments is adduced in support of their contention, but all amount to this that they are afraid the Government, having secured a large sum of money, will try to terrorize the Duma just as it terrorized the elections. The Russian Press has, unfortunately, too deep and too lasting a mistrust of its Government."

The Correspondent, of course, considered this mis-

*Times,* February 1, 1906.
**Times,* February 1, 1906.
***Times,* April 10, 1906.

trust excessive—with how little justice, events were soon to show.

A few days later, the loan was concluded—a joint Anglo-French loan, the first (I believe) in which England had participated since the Crimean War. The part played by the Foreign Office in advising the City is not easy to ascertain, but no one can doubt that our financial magnates were perfectly conscious of co-operating with the Foreign Office when they undertook to lend money to the Russian Government.*

The first Duma was opened by the Tsar on May 9, and dissolved on July 22. With its dissolution, the successful period of the Russian Revolution came to an end. Too late, *The Times* realized our mistake. Its leading article next day states that "the Government's arbitrary step, indeed, justifies only too completely those Russian reformers who besought the friends of constitutional liberty in the West not to lend more money to the autocracy.......The Russian Government obtained their loan by what now looks uncommonly like false pretences, but they cannot live on it for ever.......How can they hope to hold down for ever an exasperated people"?

The hopes of *The Times* were vain, and its penitence was brief. Step by step, the Tsar recovered his power. The more venal of his opponents were bought, the rest were dispersed to the scaffold, the gaols, and the convict settlements of Siberia. Finland was

---

*Professor Murray mocks at opponents of the Anglo-Russian Entente, by suggesting that they considered "our first step, for example, should be the subsidizing of the Russian revolutionary parties!" He does not mention that our first step was the subsidizing of their opponents, nor explain how this could be reconciled with the policy, which he advocates, of non-intervention in the internal affairs of Russia.

punished for its moment of freedom, Poland for the hundredth time tasted the bitterness of bondage, the army was reorganized, and soon the Tsar was at liberty to extend the blessings of his rule by the suppression of freedom in Persia. If the loan had been postponed for a few months, none of these results could have been achieved. Russia's gratitude is only to be secured by signal services, but fortunately for our Foreign Office the moment was one at which a signal service was possible. A Liberal Russia, which would have meant a new Europe and a new Asia, was prevented by our timely intervention.*

There can be no reasonable doubt that it was the English and French command of capital that inclined Russia to reject the offered friendship of Germany. The experience of the Western Powers during the first Moroccan crisis, in 1905, had shown them the dangers of a policy of conquest while Russia was weak: deliberately and patiently they set to work to make Russia seem strong through the suppression of liberty. If the result has proved disappointing, it can hardly be denied that England and France have

---

*There is reason to think that this is not the last occasion on which our Government defeated the hopes of Russian Liberals, as appears from the following passage in Alexinsky's "Russia and the Great War." (Fisher Unwin, 1915: p. 177): "The Russian journal *Golos*, published in Paris, stated, in its Petrograd letter, that there was a moment at the beginning of the war when Tsarism was ready to make great concessions in its domestic policy. This was the moment when Germany had already declared war upon Russia, but when the final decision of England was not yet known. The Russian Government was afraid to face Germany alone, and was conscious of its weakness; it was anxious to win the sympathies of its people. With this object in view it was actually on the point of issuing a constitutional manifesto more comprehensive than that of October 30, 1905, but at the very last moment it received the assurance that England would join in the war, and, its external situation being strengthened, Tsarism no longer thought it necessary to make concessions to the people, and the manifesto was not issued."

deserved their disappointment. It is the Russian people, the innocent victim first of repression and now of invasion, that demands our sympathy and our repentance.

After the dissolution of the first Duma, the negotiations for the Anglo-Russian Agreement continued smoothly. The only serious question at issue was the extent of Persian territory that was to be recognized as in the Russian sphere: Russia claimed the whole, but we only conceded rather more than half. In August, 1907, the Agreement was concluded, and no obstacle remained to the "peaceful penetration" of Persia.

The history of Persia since the conclusion of the Anglo-Russian Agreement is one long record of perfidy, cruelty and greed. The conduct of the Russians is closely analogous to that of the Germans in Belgium, and our conduct would have been paralleled in Belgium if we had not only brought pressure to bear on the Belgians to make them submit to German rule, but had ourselves taken Antwerp and Ostend as payment for our support of the Kaiser. Persia is a long way off, and few Englishmen have travelled there or acquired a knowledge of the Persian language. Inconvenient facts concerning such a remote country can easily be kept out of the newspapers, especially when silence serves the interest of both parties because the Government belongs to one party while its policy is that advocated by the other. Neither the English Government nor the Russian wished the truth to be known, while other civilized Powers had difficulty in ascertaining it, and no direct interest to make them interfere. The almost incredible ignorance repeatedly shown by Sir E. Grey in Persian affairs tends to prove that he left our policy in that part of the world to subordinates. But for the disinterested efforts of Professor Edward G. Browne—one of the few Englishmen who know Persia and the Persian language and literature intimately, without having any political or commercial end to serve—the facts which the English and Russian Governments wished to conceal would have been very difficult to ascertain.*

England and Russia had long been rivals in Persia, pursuing the usual method of loans to spendthrift sovereigns as a means of acquiring political influence. During the Boer War the Russians succeeded in becoming the sole creditors of Persia, which paid off a previous English loan with money borrowed from Russia. The Russians wished to absorb Persia, while we wished to keep them away from the Persian Gulf and the neighbourhood of Baluchistan. For this purpose, we supported the integrity and independence of Persia—though not to the exclusion of our ambitions in the Gulf. With the conclusion of the Anglo-Russian Entente in 1907, the rivalry of England and Russia in Persia came to an end.

The subsequent course of events is entangled in the internal affairs of Persia, and cannot be understood without some knowledge of the struggle between the

---

*I have derived my knowledge of these facts largely from three pamphlets by Professor Browne, namely:

A brief narrative of events in Persia, followed by an Appendix on the Persian Constitution.   Luzac & Co., 46, Great Russell Street, W. C., 1909.

The Persian Crisis of December, 1911; how it arose and whither it may lead us.   Compiled for the use of the Persia Committee.   Privately printed.   New Year's Day, 1912.

The Reign of Terror at Tabriz:   England's responsibility. With photographs and a brief narrative of the events of December, 1911, and January, 1912.   Compiled for the use of the Persia Committee.   October, 1912.

I am compelled to suppose that Professor Murray has not seen these pamphlets.   If he had, it seems impossible that he should have dealt with the Persian question as he has dealt with it, being, as he is, a man conspicuous for humane feeling and hatred of cruelty and oppression.

The third of the above pamphlets is the subject of a memorandum by Mr. Shipley (our Consul in Tabriz), No. 464 (p. 230), in The Blue Book Persia, No. 1 (1913, Cd. 6807.   This memorandum is intended to mitigate the force of Professor Browne's indictment, but fails entirely in its object.

Mr. Shuster's book, "The Strangling of Persia" (Fisher Unwin, 1912), is very important to all who wish to understand the Persian question.

Constitutionalists and the Shah, which began in 1906
and continued until we procured the final defeat of
the Constitutionalists in 1911.

The Shah's extravagances had led him to need
money, and the need of money had made him subservient to Russia in order to get loans.  His sub-
servience to Russia, and his misgovernment, had
roused a continually growing opposition in Persia,
which was encouraged in its hope of independence by
the Japanese victory in the war of 1904-5, and by the
subsequent revolution in Russia.  The English, at that
time still more or less hostile to Russia owing to the
Japanese Alliance, showed sympathy with the Persian nationalists.  In July, 1906, as the result of conflicts between the people and the soldiers, the malcon-
tents asked and obtained asylum in the gardens of
the British Legation in Teheran, at first in small
numbers, but finally to the number of 15,000.  They
demanded a Parliament, and the Shah, on August
5, 1906, issued a proclamation agreeing to grant their
request.  The Assembly met on October 7.  It proceeded at once to the consideration of much-needed
reforms, in which it appears to have shown judgment
and patriotism.  Its first Budget, which was presented
in 1907, undertook the task of converting the annual
deficit into a surplus, which was vitally necessary
if foreign influence was to be diminished.  Since it
was not practicable to effect this by increasing the
revenue, it had to be effected by diminishing the expenditure, and among the items that were cut down
was the Shah's Civil List.  This, though he had sworn
repeatedly to observe the Constitution, increased the

hostility which he had never ceased to feel. Nevertheless, if no foreign influence had intervened, the Nationalists could have easily continued, as before, to get the better of all the efforts of this perjured tyrant.

But meanwhile the Anglo-Russian Agreement had been concluded (August 31, 1907), with its English and Russian spheres. This division into spheres naturally alarmed the Persians, in spite of the recognition of the integrity and independence of Persia. To their inquiry whether it was intended to partition Persia, our Minister replied, with the knowledge and co-operation of the Russian Legation, by the following official communication:

"Information has reached me that the report is rife in Persia that the result of the Agreement concluded between England and Russia will be the intervention of these two Powers in Persia, and the partition of Persia between them. Your Excellency is aware that the negotiations between England and Russia are of a wholly different character, since the Mushiru 'l-Mulk recently visited both St. Petersburg and London, and discussed the matter with the Ministers for Foreign Affairs of both Powers, who explicitly declared to him the objects aimed at by their represtive Governments in Persia, which assurance he has no doubt duly reported.

"Sir Edward Grey has informed me of the substance of his conversations with the Mushiru 'l-Mulk, and also of the substance of M. Isvolsky's declarations, officially communicated to the British Government.

"Sir Edward Grey informs me that he has explained to the Mushiru 'l-Mulk that he and M. Isvolsky are completely in accord on two fundamental points.

"Firstly, neither of the two Powers will interfere in the affairs of Persia unless injury is inflicted on the persons and property of their subjects.

"Secondly, negotiations arising out of the Anglo-Russian Agreement must not violate the integrity and independence of Persia.

"Sir Edward Grey also observes that hitherto antagonism has existed between England and Russia, each of whom has endeavoured to prevent the continuance of the other in Persia, and had this antagonism been prolonged in the present uncertain state of Persia, one or both of these two Powers might have been tempted to interfere in the internal affairs of Persia, so as not to allow the other to profit by the existing state of things, or to profit by it to the detriment of others. The object of the present negotiations between England and Russia is to prevent such difficulties from arising between them, and these negotiations are in truth in no wise directed against Persia, as M. Isvolsky has clearly explained to the Mushiru'l-Mulk, saying, 'Neither of the two Powers seeks anything from Persia, so that Persia can concentrate all her energies on the settlement of her internal affairs'. Both Ministers are entirely in accord as to the policy of non-intervention in Persia, and have left no possible ground for doubt in the matter. M. Isvolsky's words, which include the intentions of England are as follows: 'Russia's general principle will be to refrain from any kind of intervention in the internal affairs of other countries so long as nothing injurious to her interests is done; and it is quite impossible that she should deviate from this principle in this present case.'

"As to the reported partition of Persia between Russia and England, concerning which it is asserted that the two Powers above-mentioned wish to define spheres of influence for themselves, Sir E. Grey and M. Isvolsky have explicitly declared that these reports have no foundation. What the two Powers desire is to come to an agreement which will prevent future difficulties and disputes from arising, by guaranteeing that neither Power will aim at acquiring influence in those parts of Persia which are adjacent to the frontier of the other. This agreement is injurious neither to the interests of Persia nor to those of any other foreign nation, since it binds only England and Russia not to embark on any course of action in Persia calculated to injure the interests of the other, and so in the future to deliver Persia from those demands which in the past have proved so injurious to the progress of her political aspirations. This is what M. Isvolsky says:

" 'This Agreement between the two European Powers which have the greatest interests in Persia, based as it is on a guarantee of her independence and integrity, can only serve to further and promote Persian interests, for henceforth Persia, aided and assisted by these two powerful neighbouring States, can employ all her powers in internal reforms.'

"From the above statements you will see how baseless and unfounded are these rumours which have lately prevailed in Persia concerning the political ambitions of England and Russia in this country. The object of the two Powers in making this Agreement is not in any way to attack, but rather to assure forever the independence of Persia. Not only do they not wish to have at hand any excuse for intervention, but their object in these friendly negotiations *was not to allow one another to intervene* on the pretext of safeguarding their interests. The two Powers hope that in the future Persia will be forever delivered from the fear of foreign intervention, and will thus be perfectly free to manage her own affairs in her own way, whereby advantage will accrue both to herself and to the whole world.''

Nevertheless, within a few years, more than half of Persia had been absorbed by Russia, and more than half the remainder had come under our power.

When questions were asked in the House about this declaration, it appeared that Sir Edward Grey had no knowledge of it.*

About the end of February, 1908, three men, who were never caught, threw a bomb at the Shah's automobile when the Shah was in another carriage. The chauffeur was killed. Whether the bomb was thrown by extremists of the Constitutional party, or by adherents of the Shah in order to promote a reaction, is not known. On June 2, three months later, the Russian Minister, supported apparently by the British Chargé d'Affaires, told the Persian Foreign Secretary that

''The life of the Shah is in jeopardy. What busi-

---

*December 14, 1911. Mr. Acland, the Under-Secretary, had expressed equal ignorance on December 5. Professor Murray makes no mention of this Declaration.

ness have these Nationalists to interfere with His Majesty's personal servants, especially the old Amir Bahadur Zang, who watches over his master's safety like a faithful watch-dog? The *anjumans* and Nationalists have transgressed all bounds, and now wish to depose the Shah. This we cannot tolerate, and should it happen, Russia will be compelled to interfere, and will do so with the approval and sanction of England.''

In view of these threats, the Nationalist leaders decided that it would be useless to resist the Shah by force of arms, since the only result would be foreign intervention. Meanwhile, the Shah, emboldened by Russian support, adopted a more vigorous policy. The very next day (June 3) he departed from the city to the ''Shah's Garden'' outside the walls, where he was less amenable to popular pressure. On June 5, he treacherously arrested some leading Nationalists whom he had invited to confer with him. On June 28 he caused his Cossacks, under their Russian Colonel Liakhoff, to plant artillery round the Assembly, shoot down those who attempted to defend it, and disperse the remainder. In Teheran he was completely victorious, and for a time the hopes of the Nationalist movement seemed at an end.

But outside the capital the supporters of the Parliament proved more difficult to suppress. Especially Tabriz, in the north, near the Russian border, offered a vigorous resistance, and in April, 1909, was still withstanding a siege by the Shah's troops. It was said that the European Consuls in Tabriz were in danger, and on this ground Russian troops crossed the border, raised the siege and encamped just outside the town, where, until they occupied the town itself in December, 1911, they stayed in spite of the fact that (at any rate in the opinion of the British Government) there was no valid excuse for their remaining.

The Russian intervention at Tabriz saved the Nationalist cause at that time, but this was of course no part of the motive with which it was undertaken. Sir Arthur Nicholson, then our Ambassador at Petrograd, now permanent Under-Secretary for Foreign Affairs, expressed the official view of both Governments. "It seems to me," he wrote, "that it would be the Nationalists who would profit by the arrival of the Russian force, but I submit that the chief object to be kept in view is the safety of the Consuls, even at the risk of the measures which circumstances have rendered necessary proving of benefit to the popular movement at Tabriz." Sir Arthur Nicholson was quite right. For the moment, the Russians regretfully saved the Nationalist cause; but their troops at Tabriz proved themselves capable, when the time came, of striking a blow against human liberty which must have surpassed even that astute diplomatist's expectations.

The Nationalist's cause prospered, and in July, 1909, the Shah's Cossacks were defeated, Teheran was occupied and the Shah deposed.*

---

*These Cossacks were under Russian officers, who, according to the *Times'* Correspondent, were "completely under the control of the Russian Government, owing to the fact that their pensions and their prospect of future re-instatement depend on their acting in accordance with the wishes of St. Petersburg." Professor Browne points out that Sir E. Grey did not know of the unsuccessful resistance of the Shah's Cossacks to the Nationalists, but stated on three separate occasions (July 27, November 27, and December 14, 1911), that if their Russian officers "had interfered or lifted a finger, and used their influence in Teheran, the Shah would never have been expelled."

A Protocol was signed in August, 1909, between the Persian Government on the one hand, and the Russian and British Governments on the other hand, by which the Persians agreed to pay the ex-Shah a pension of £16,666 a year, while Russia agreed to prevent him from conducting any political agitation against Persia. If Russia failed to prevent this, Persia was to be free to stop his pension.** This contract, as we shall see, was treated by Russia as a "scrap of paper."

In the time which followed, the Russians increased the number of their troops in Persia, fomented disorder as an excuse for intervention, and with our help prevented the Persian Government from borrowing the money required to suppress disorder, unless on terms which would have meant a virtual loss of independence.

In November, 1910, Russia and Germany concluded the Potsdam Agreement, which gave Russia a free hand in Persia. This strengthened Russia's hands, not only by removing German opposition, but also by making England fear that Russia was being attracted into "the orbit of a single diplomacy", as Sir E. Grey expressed it. From this time on, we became completely subservient to Russia in Persia, since we lived

---

**The crucial article of the Protocol is Article II, which says: "The two representatives (i. e., the British Minister and the Russian Chargé de'Affairs), undertake to give His Majesty Mohammed Ali Mirza strict injunctions to abstain in future from all political agitation against Persia, and the Imperial Russian Government promise on their side to take all effective steps in order to prevent any such agitation on his part. If His Majesty Mohammed Ali Mirza leaves Russia, and if it is proved to the satisfaction of the two legations that in any country other than Russia he has carried on political agitation against Persia, the Persian Government shall have the right to cease payment of his pension."—Cd. 5120.

in terror of a *rapprochement* between the Tsar and the Kaiser.*

A few days before the conclusion of the Potsdam Agreement, the Persian Foreign Minister informed the English and Russian Legations that he had discovered a treasonable correspondence of the ex-Shah with some frontier tribes, and that he proposed to stop that noble exile's allowance while the facts were investigated.    The English and Russians refused to investigate the charges, and caused the Persian Minister to be shadowed like a criminal until the money was paid.    He had been educated in England, and was suspected of Anglophil tendencies; by the end of December, he was forced to resign.    Meanwhile the ex-Shah left Russia and began organizing preparations for the invasion which he made in 1911, entering Persia from Russia by a Russian boat on the Caspian.    This expedition led to a Civil War in which the ex-Shah and his partisans were defeated. But even after this the Persian Government was forced to continue to pay him a pension.*

The situation of Persia at this time was difficult, but not yet hopeless.    The Persians have been recognized throughout Islam as the most civilized of Mahometan races, and as the leader in poetry, philos-

---

*For the effect of the Potsdam Agreement on Persia and on British policy in connection with Persia, see Shuster, "The Strangling of Persia," pp. 226 ff.

*Professor Murray says:—"I see no reason to suspect the Russian Government of having connived at this enterprise," namely the ex-Shah's invasion.    But "when once the Shah had landed, Russia was not disposed to suppress him.    She had put down one Royalist rebellion after another, when the constitutional Government had been unable to cope with them.    She had by nature no liking for Constitutionalists as against anointed Kings, and she proposed to Great Britain to let the Shah have his chance and then support whatever Government

ophy and art. The country, however, contains many tribes who are more warlike and less civilized than the true Persians. The genuine constitutional enthusiasm which was almost universal among the true Persians—except for a few who had some private interest in the old régime—was naturally beyond the mental capacity of most of the tribes. They took one side or the other for motives which had little to do with the issue of constitutionalism versus absolutism. The Government could have kept order if it could have got money, but this the English and Russian Governments prevented. The consequent partial failure of the Constitutionalists to keep order was used by Russia and England as an excuse for fresh interventions and fresh military occupations; ever since April, 1909, the Russians had troops in the north, whose numbers were increased from time to time, and in October, 1911, we began landing Indian troops at Bushire.*

At the request of the Persian Government, an American financial mission was despatched in 1911 under the leadership of Mr. Shuster, an American financial official in the Philippines. Mr. Shuster's mission, which had to deal with a very complicated state of affairs, seemed at first to promise the regener-

---

proved to have the greatest hold on the country. Great Britain maintained firmly that he could not be recognized." The Protocol of August, 1909, is not mentioned by Professor Murray: no one could guess from his account that the attitude which he confesses to have been that of Russia constituted a breach of faith, though this appears even from the Blue Books (e. g. Cd. 6104, Nos. 218, 244). It is fairly clear that Russia desired disorders in Persia, as an excuse for intervention. What Russia seems to have feared most was a definitive victory for either party before her own schemes had matured.

*Cd. 6105, No. 75 (p. 32).

ation of Persia, but brought about instead the final
catastrophe. Mr. Shuster and his coadjutors began
their task of financial organization in May, 1911.
They were dismissed as the result of a Russian ultimatum presented on November 29, 1911. Everything
possible has been done by *The Times*, Sir E. Grey
and Professor Murray to represent Mr. Shuster as
an impracticable and tactless idealist, whom the Russians could not have been expected to endure. The
charges against him, when carefully analyzed, amount
to three: (1) that he devoted himself whole-heart-
edly to the interests of Persia; (2) that his policy
was calculated to restore order and independence to
Persia; (3) that he supposed the Russians capable
of some respect for their promises. All these charges
have been proved up to the hilt; and all right-minded
people will therefore agree that he was unfit for his
post.*

In order to be able to collect taxes, Mr. Shuster set
to work to organize a gendarmerie, of which he offered the command to Major Stokes of the Indian

---

*An interesting conversation between M. Nératof and our
Chargé d'Affaires in Petrograd, took place on October 19, 1911.
"I (Mr. O'Beirne) reminded M. Nératof that Russia had recently
vetoed the various proposals put forward with the object of
enabling the Persian Government to restore order in the country
—proposals which, for our part, we had welcomed as affording
some hope of an improvement in the state of things in the
south. Russia had objected to these proposals, but she had suggested nothing to take their place. I begged His Excellency
to tell me frankly what it was that the Russian Government
wished done.

"M. Nératof replied that the first thing necessary was that
Mr. Shuster should understand that he must act in concert with,
and in accordance with the interests of, Russia, and of course, His
Excellency added, of Great Britain also. The Persian reforms
must be proceeded with gradually and in such a manner as to
take Russian interests into account. *It must be remembered
that the question was not merely one of the good of Persia, but
also of the special position of Russia.*"
(My italics. Cd. 6105, No. 45, p. 19. Cf. *ib.*, No. 56.)

Army. Russia objected, on the ground that no Englishman must be allowed authority in the Russian
sphere, and the gendarmerie would have to operate
in the Russian sphere as well as elsewhere. Means
were found by the British Government to bring pressure to bear on Major Stokes* and he resigned. Mr.
Shuster's appointment of a British subject, Mr.
Lecoffre, as his agent in Tabriz was made a ground
of complaint by Russia—not unnaturally, since Russia's conduct in Tabriz shortly afterwards was such
as Englishmen must not witness if it could be prevented. (It must be remembered that the Russians
had no rights in Tabriz except those of conquest—
the very same that the Germans have in Belgium).
But these difficulties could perhaps have been overcome; at any rate it was not through them that the
Russians finally asserted themselves.**

A brother of the ex-Shah, Shoa-es-Sultaneh, had
taken part in the recent rebellion, and his property
was declared confiscated by the Persian Government.
But the Russian Bank asserted that his house was
mortgaged to them, and objected to Mr. Shuster's
attempt to take possession of it. The Persian Government protested against the action of the Russian Consul-General, who sent Russian Cossacks to
the house with threats that they would fire on the

---

*See Cd. 6105, No. 209 (p. 89) ; Cf. *ib.*, No. 97 (p. 40).
**Sir E. Grey regretted that the Russians did not base
their interference upon the appointment of Mr Lecoffre at
Tabriz.   The reply of the Russian Government is interesting.
"M. Nératof pointed out that from a formal point of view, it
would be difficult for them to protest against appointments such
as that of Mr. Lecoffre to Tabriz, since such a protest would
constitute an interference in the internal affairs of Persia."
Cd. 6105, No. 113 (p. 46).   Mr. Shuster's excellent grounds for
the appointment of Mr. Lecoffre are given in the same Blue
Book, No. 89.

Persian gendarmes.  The incidents of the dispute are differently related by the two sides:* they are complicated, and I have not the means of sifting the evidence.  The dispute ended in the Russians presenting two successive ultimatums, which put an end to what remained of Persian liberty.

The dispute about the house arose on October 9, and on October 10 it appeared to be closed owing to the Russian Minister dissociating himself from the Consul-General.  But this appearance was deceptive. On November 2, the Russian Minister presented an ultimatum, demanding the removal of the gendarmes from the house, and an apology from the Persian Government.  The Persian Government accepted the ultimatum, but Mr. Shuster and the Majlis resisted it.  Although the Persian Foreign Minister tendered the required apology for an offence which, according to Persian accounts, had never been committed, the

---

*Professor Murray's account is as follows:—"The final clash came in a curious manner.  Mr. Shuster had decided—not unjustly, as far as one can judge—to confiscate the large estates of a brother of the ex-Shah, Shoa-es-Sultaneh.  Part of this prince's property was a house which was mortgaged to the Russian Bank—or so at least the Bank claimed—and which lay close to the Russian Consulate.  Now Russians engaged in commerce and the Consular service seem, naturally enough, to have less sense of correct behaviour or less control over their feelings than ministers and diplomats.  And when Mr. Shuster's Treasury Officials came to seize this house the Russian Consul sent men to drive them away, and is said to have been reprimanded by his Minister for doing so.  Mr. Shuster immediately sent one gendarme with an explanation to the Consulate and a hundred gendarmes with rifles to the mortgaged house.  There was resistance and some trouble, and, instead of apologizing, or negotiating, or attempting a compromise, Mr. Shuster, through the Cabinet, demanded the recall of the Russian Consul-General." Even in this account, the excuse seems hardly adequate for destroying a nation's freedom.  This was also Sir E. Grey's view: "I said it was unfortunate, in the first instance that the Russian ultimatum had been based upon the question of the property of the Shoa-es-Sultaneh for the question was of comparatively slight importance, and the Russian case with regard to it did not seem to me very strong."  (Cd. 6105, No. 212, p. 90; cf. *ib.*, No. 109, p. 45).

Russians presented a second ultimatum (November 29) demanding (1) the dismissal of Mr. Shuster and Mr. Lecoffre; (2) an undertaking not in future to appoint foreigners in the Government service without the consent of Russia and England;* and (3) the payment of an indemnity** covering the expenses of the Russian expedition sent against Persia at the time of the first ultimatum, and not recalled or arrested in its march when the first ultimatum was accepted. Mr. Shuster and the Majlis continued to hold out, but the Persian Government was compelled to yield. Mr. Shuster was dismissed, the Majlis came to an end, and Persian liberty was killed.

It has been made an accusation against Mr. Shuster that he was anti-Russian.* It would be exactly as rational to blame the Belgian Government for being anti-German. The Anglo-Russian Agreement, since Persia was not a party to it, gave the Russians no

---

*This was the demand which the Persian Government was the most reluctant to yield, since it constituted a sacrifice of independence. Both the English and the Russian Governments maintained that it only embodied the principle of the Anglo-Russian Agreeemnt and the practice since its conclusion." (Cd. 6105, Nos. 168, 243; but Russia finally agreed to a slight modification in this demand, *ib.*, Nos. 273, 288, and Cd. 6264, No. 88, Enclosures 1 and 2).

**This was the only one of the three demands that Sir E. Grey objected to. Professor Murray speaks of it as "the only cruel part" of Russia's demands.

*Professor Murray's remarks on this subject are curious. "He considered himself the servant of an independent Persia." "Mr. Shuster happened to be both a very headstrong and a prejudiced Russophobe. He acted like the head of an independent kingdom." He "made no concealment of his detestation of Russia." After the second ultimatum, "By the time the (Russian) troops had reached Kasvin the ultimatum was accepted, and a few weeks later Mr. Shuster had left Persia. It ought to have been mentioned that he had spent part of his scanty leisure in writing a fierce anti-Russian pamphlet, which was translated into Persian and circulated broadcast." This was his letter to "The Times" of Oct. 21, 1911, which is reprinted as an Appendix in his book, "The Strangling of Persia", 1912, pp. 313-326.

rights in Persia. If there had been an Anglo-German Agreement to partition Belgium, that would not have given the Germans or us any rights against the Government of Belgium. If the Persian Government chose to appoint Englishmen in the Russian sphere, it had a perfect right to do so.** Only four years earlier, in 1907, our Minister in Teheran had issued his declaration explaining that the purpose of the Anglo-Russian Agreement was to facilitate the maintenance of Persian integrity and independence. Russia, deliberately and persistently worked to absorb the northern half of Persia. Whatever may have been the intentions of the Government in Petrograd,* the methods of Russian officials in Persia and on the frontier were the reverse of scrupulous, involving, as they did, the encouragement of disorder, brigandage and dissension, not to mention the breach of faith in regard to the ex-Shah. In opposing the Russians, Mr. Shuster was adopting a counsel of despair; but there could be no hope for Persia if Russia were not opposed.** And it is impossible to escape the conclusion that the real grievance against Mr. Shuster was the hope of Persian regeneration which his vigour

---

**This was recognized by Russia, as appears from the statement of M. Nératof quoted above (Cd. 6105, No. 113).

*I do not think the Government in Petrograd can be absolved. Whoever doubts this should read the correspondence as to the second ultimatum in Cd. 6105, and the correspondence on the subject of a loan to Persia in Cd. 6807. In discussing the Anglo-Russian Agreement of 1907, Professor Murray says: "It is clear that, if honestly carried out, it did not increase but greatly limited the freedom of the two Powers to interfere wih Persia." It would seem to follow that Professor Murray must think that the Agreement was *not* "honestly carried out", for it was constantly invoked as a general ground for interference when Mr. Shuster, Major Stokes, and Mr. Lecoffre were being dismissed by Russia's fiat.

**See Mr. Shuster's book, "The Strangling of Persia."

and honesty inspires. I was early offered," he said, "the plain choice between serving the Persian people and only appearing to do so, while actually serving foreign interests bent on Persia's natural destruction. I have no apologies to offer for my course." I do not think any unbiassed person can avoid the conclusion that Mr. Shuster was in the right, that Russia was brutal and tortuous, and that England was subservient and willing to profit by Russia's crime.

At the end of December, 1911, the Russian troops, who had been stationed just outside Tabriz since April, 1909, entered the city and established a reign of terror.* They began by hanging eight of the leading nationalists, including the chief Mullah of Azerbaijan, the Sikat-el-Islam, whose position corresponded to that of Cardinal Mercier.** It is said that he was anti-Russian, and, if so, of course he deserved to die. After they had executed these eight men, they admitted Samad Khan Shuja-ud-Dowleh, the man who had been leading the partisans of the ex-Shah in their attacks on Tabriz.* With their ap-

---

*The best evidence for what occurred at this time is that of Mr. G. D. Turner, then of the Indian Y. M. C. A., now in the British army in France. He happened, in the course of missionary work, to be in Tabriz shortly after this time, and while there he obtained photographs of atrocities, some of which are reproduced in Professor Browne's "Reign of Terror in Tabriz". The other evidence is mainly that of Persian refugees. (This evidence is more or less open to question, but is as good as the evidence on which much of the Bryce report is based.) On this evidence, see a letter from Professor Browne to the Manchester Guardian on February 9, 1912; the same paper, on September 3, 1912, printed a communication from Mr. Turner giving his evidence. What follows is from these sources. The account in the Blue Books is hopelessly inadequate.

**Our Ambassador in Petrograd spoke of the execution of the Sikat-el-Islam to M. Sazonof as "a most unfortunate occurrence as well as a grave blunder". Cd. 6264, No. 52.

*He was superseded later, though Russia pressed for his retention.

proval and that of the British Consul in Tabriz, this
man became *de facto* Governor of Tabriz, and proceeded to show what resolute government could do.
The Russians did nothing to interfere with Shuja's
activities, and the British Consul did not report his
atrocities. A few samples of what occurred must
suffice.

"Mirza Mahmud of Salmas, one of the *Ulema* and
one of those elected in the elections of the first degree
to membership of the Majlis, was put to death in the
house of Samad Khan with all sorts of torments.
While he was still alive they plucked out his eyes and
cut out his tongue (for he was an orator), after which
they slew him. Samad Khan offered to let him go
on payment of 400 tomans, but this sum he neither
possessed nor could obtain."

"Amongst the victims were two young lads named
Hasan and Kadir, aged 18 and 12 respectively, whose
only fault was that their elder brothers, who were
national volunteers, had succeeded in escaping across
the Turkish frontier, where they are still wander-
ing, hungry and starved with cold."

"He (Samad Khan) beheaded Na'il Yusef of
Hukmabad and afterwards cut his body in two halves
like a sheep, and suspended them on either side of
the bazaar."*

The foregoing quotations are from Nationalist
refugees, and might therefore be doubted except

---

*Photographs of the two halves are published by Professor
Browne in "The Reign of Terror in Tabriz". These are not
mentioned by Professor Murray, who says: "According to
Nationalist statements, they cut this man (the chief Mullah,
not Na'il Yusef), in two pieces and marched between them into
the citadel." This statement gives no hint that the evidence
for what really did occur is conclusive.

where the photographs obtained by Mr. Turner support them. What follows is all from Mr. Turner's statement.

"The relinquishment of rifle and bayonet was only the signal for the appearance of the gallows. Even before the installation of the Russians as Governor on December 30th, of Samad Khan Shuja-ud-Dowleh the hangings begans, and Russia is responsible not only for those carried out by her own officers but for those nominally directed by their appointed Governor. Nor can we hold Russia free from the responsibility for atrocities perpetuated by this same Governor, such as beating men to death in water ponds, sewing up the mouths of certain who had spoken in favour of the Constitution, nailing horseshoes on men's feet and driving them through the bazaar, and other unspeakable barbarities. Since last December the life of no man who was even supposed to be in favour of the Constitution has been safe, no matter how honourable his character or how high his position.

"The Sikat-ul-Islam was the chief Moslem ecclesiastic in Tabriz. He was a man of very unusual ability, of great personal charm, and singularly broadminded. He was on excellent terms not only with his co-religionists but with the Christians of the city. Early in December he had called on the British Consul to ask if he might seek protection in the Consulate in the event of danger to himself; the reply was that unless he was in some immediate danger the Consulate could not promise protection. He called also at the Russian Consulate and was assured that whatever happened his safety would be respected. In the disturbances already described he took no part whatever, although he was in sympathy with the Constitution and the struggle for Persian independence. Nevertheless he was seized by the Russians, his house was searched for a list of men in favour of Constitutional Government, and a large sum of money extracted from him in return for a promise of his liberty.

"His trial followed, and I am told on good authority that it consisted of his being asked if he had written to a friend in Urumiah a letter something to the following effect: 'The Russians have attacked us and we have resisted them, so far effectively. We trust that you will do the same.' On admitting that it was his letter, he was dragged off to the gallows. The gallows, as one can see in a photograph in my possession, was gaily painted like a barber's pole with Russian colours. Eight were hung together, the Sikat-ul-Islam in the middle and lowest of all. The Persian servants employed as hangmen by the Russians refused to do their work in his case, until they were brutally beaten by Russian officers with their knouts. The Russian officers are to be seen standing in front of the bodies posing for their photograph....... It should be added that this execution took place without the knowledge of the English Consul, probably to avoid a protest on his part."

"Some of those hung were known personally to Europeans in Tabriz, who are positive that they took no part in the fighting. They were hung simply because they were constitutionalists, although the charge

brought against them probably was that they incited
or encouraged the Fidais to resistance.''

Shuja ud-Dowleh, who was *de facto* Governor, and
directed events after the first day of the Russian
occupation, was objected to by the Persian Government. Both the Russians and the English urged the
Persians to appoint him formally as Governor, even
after all his atrocities had been committed. Thus
Sir E. Grey telegraphed, on February 25, 1912, to
the British Minister at Teheran: ''Is there any
prospect, in view of our combined action concerning the ex-Shah, of obtaining the consent of the Persian Government to the appointment of Shuja-ud-
Dowleh to the post of Governor-General; and, if so,
what confidence could they place in his loyalty to
them?''* Finally the objections of the Persian
Government were allowed to prevail, and another
Governor was appointed, with Shuja as his assistant.

Russian and British action extinguished the hopes
of Persia, and it is not easy to see how they can be
revived. A victorious Germany would, no doubt, at
first proclaim itself the protector of Islam, and might
temporarily restore Persian independence. But a
Germany established in Mesopotamia and on the Persian Gulf would soon begin to treat Persia as Russia
has treated it. All the Great Powers, in their dealings with weak nations, are predatory and brutal.
In criticizing Russian action in Persia, I do not wish
to suggest that Germany would have acted better; I
wish only to make it clear that the guiding principles

---

*Cd. 6264, No. 232 (p. 96). It is clear that Sir E. Grey did
not know how Shuja had been behaving.

of European policy, in Asia as in Africa, are such as must bring horror and dismay to every man with a spark of humanity in his nature.*    The only hope for Persia, as for the rest of Asia, seems to lie in such a weakening of all the Great Powers of Europe, either in this war or in the subsequent wars foretold by Professors here and in Germany,** as shall enable the more backward nations to throw off the yoke fastened on them by the Cabinets and financiers of "civilized" States.    There is indeed another possibility: some glimmering of justice and humanity might conceivably appear in the external policy of the Powers. But this cannot happen so long as their worst acts are whitewashed by their best citizens.    So long as we continue to know the faults of our enemies, and to be ignorant of the faults of our friends and ourselves, it is possible for men who have no bad desires to join in the hatred produced by pride and fear, and to contribute, against their will, to the forces of antagonism which stand in the way of a better spirit. Righteousness cannot be born until self-righteousness is dead.

----

**Cf. Professor Ridgeway as reported in *The Times*, 7th May, 1915, who is reported as having said: "Far from this being the last war, the hard facts pointed rather to its being the first of a vast series of struggles different from those yet known"; and in an exactly similar sense, Eduard Meyer in "Scientia", March, 1915.

## V. WHAT OUR POLICY OUGHT TO
## HAVE BEEN

It is more difficult to say what we ought to have
done than to see, now that war has come, that what
we did was not the best possible. The most effective
defence of Sir E. Grey consists in pointing to German aggressiveness and German strength and asking
how otherwise it could have been met.* To this
there are answers of details, and there is a broad
answer which challenges the whole spirit and purpose of the foreign policy pursued by all the Great
Powers of Europe.

Beginning with answers of detail, we find that
England, on various occasions, pursued a policy of
quite needless hostility to Germany, and acted in a
way which was ideally suited to increase the hold
of militarism and aggression on German public
opinion. How we acted in regard to Morocco has
already been shown. In helping to suppress the Russian revolution, we were not only committing a crime
against Russia, a crime against liberty, and a crime
against humanity, but we were preventing the removal of the chief argument by which the military

---

*This is the defence with which Pofessor Murray concludes
his pamphlet. Speaking of Sir Edward Grey's policy in Persia,
he says: "As a Liberal and a reasonable man, I cannot condemn it, though I admit that it has failed to achieve its full
object." And again, after enumerating various views with which
neither he nor I agree, he says: "All these classes of politician
have a right to attack and denounce Sir Edward Grey for his
policy in Persia, but Liberals, as far as I can see, have no
right." This line of defence is by far the strongest, but I do
not think it will bear careful examination.

party have appealed to the ordinary citizen in Germany. Militarists everywhere base their appeal upon fear: powerful neighbors, they say, are ready to attack us, and unless we are prepared we shall be overwhelmed. The chief bogey used by German militarists for this purpose was Russia. If the Russian revolution had been successful, this bogey would have ceased to be efficacious, and a Liberal movement in Germany would have had a far better chance of success. By rehabilitating the Russian autocracy, we took one of the surest means of reinforcing German militarism.

Our opposition to German Colonial expansion was another source of encouragement to German aggressiveness.* Apart from the Moroccan question, there was the Bagdad Railway question, which had a profound influence upon the fate of Persia. We opposed the railway, and German enterprise in Mesopotamia, because it was intended that the railway, under German control, should have a terminus on the Persian Gulf, where we considered that we had special interests on account of India. It was supposed that a German naval base on the Gulf would constitute a strategic danger to our naval command of the Indian Ocean. On this ground, we opposed the railway unless it were either internationalised or not allowed to extend south of Bagdad. At first

*Professor Murray quotes Sir Edward Grey's speech of Nov. 27, 1911, in which he stated that we did not wish to indulge in a dog-in-the-manger policy, or to oppose German desires for an extension of territory by friendly arrangement, but that there were certain places which, on account of British interests, we should not wish to see in other hands. In practice, however, these places have been found, since 1904, to include all places that Germany in fact desired.

the Russians also opposed it, but after the Potsdam Agreement of 1910, they withdrew their opposition in return for a free hand in Persia. If we had been the first to withdraw our opposition, we could, if we had wished, have procured a *quid pro quo* which would have been a gain, and not a loss, to the general interests of mankind. We could, for example, have demanded German support in maintaining the independence and integrity of Persia. The strategical danger which we feared was purely imaginary: so long as the Germans did not secure command of the sea, anything which caused them to divide their Navy was an advantage to us, as has been shown by the fate of their Pacific fleet. But on account of this imaginery danger, we opposed their colonial ambitions, and drove them to acquiesce in Russia's Persian crimes.

Another example of the recklessness with which we allowed our relations with Germany to become embittered is the Naval Scare of 1909, which, though not connected with the Foreign Office, had such an influence on Anglo-German friction as to require mention.*

In that year, Mr. McKenna, in his official statement as First Lord of the Admiralty, accused the German Government of secretly accelerating their naval programme, and of being able to construct eight Dreadnoughts at once instead of four, which

---

*Accounts of this scare may be read in G. H. Perris, "Our Foreign Policy and Sir Edward Grey's Failure" and "The War Traders: an Exposure"; Hirst, "The Six Panics"; J. T. Walton Newbould, "How Asquith Helped the Armour Ring" (National Labour Press, 1d.); "Armaments and Patriotism," 6 articles in the "Daily News" for May, 1913.

was their official figure. We were told that they could
build ships more quickly than we could, and that
we ran a risk of being inferior to them at sea during
the year 1912. Mr. McKenna estimated that in
April, 1912, they would have 17 Dreadnoughts; Mr.
Balfour estimated that they would have 21 or 25. By
the middle of 1912, they had in fact 13. It was stated
that Krupp's had increased the number of their em-
ployees since January, 1907, from 64,000 to 100,000,
when in fact, as appeared from ''The Times'' of
January 4, 1910, there had been a slight decrease in
the number during the two years from January, 1907,
to January, 1909. The accusation of trickery against
the German Government was made the basis of a
terrific alarmist campaign, by our Government and
still more by Mr. Balfour, the present First Lord of
the Admiralty, according to whom it was too late to
secure our naval supremacy in the year 1912, and we
could only be meek and hope the Germans would do
nothing until we had again caught them up. His
lugubrious joy was part of the campaign against the
''People's Budget,'' and was carried on throughout
the General Election of January, 1910.

The ''facts'' upon which the Government based its
Navy Estimates in 1909 were wholly false,* and, as
the Government itself was subsequently forced to
confess, the actual numbers of German Dreadnoughts

---

*Professor Murray on the subject of the scare says: ''There
were great suspicions of secret shipbuilding in this year and the
next, and in 1909 facts which came to the knowledge of Mr.
McKenna, the First Lord of the Admiralty, made him demand
an unusual increase of the British programme. His fears were,
as a matter of fact, not realised, though the statements of fact
which he made were quite accurate.'' Professor Murray does
not mention Mr. Mulliner, the hero of the melodrama.

in the following years fell far short of the numbers expected by our Admiralty.** As is customary in such cases, the Government did not reveal the source of its information. Fortunately the man who had informed them of our danger himself boasted, later on, of the part he had played in saving the Empire.***

The man from whom the Government derived its information was Mr. Mulliner, the enterprising Managing Director of the Coventry Ordnance Works, a firm which obtained fewer orders from the Admiralty than it thought it deserved. On March 3, Mr. Mulliner gave evidence before the Cabinet as to the enormous acceleration in Germany in the production of armaments, and particularly of guns and gun-mountings. On March 16, Mr. McKenna introduced the Naval Estimates, in a speech based upon Mr. Mulliner's evidence. He asked for an increase of nearly £3,000,000, on the ground that Germany was trying to steal a march on us and to emerge suddenly with a Navy stronger than ours. The House of Commons was not told that these statements rested upon the assertions of an individual with a strong financial interest in the increased production of naval guns. In England, most men accepted the statements as gospel. The German Government, which knew them to be false, very naturally supposed that our Government wished to produce a quarrel. No doubt our Government was deceived; but the Germans were pardonable if they supposed it less simple-minded than it was.

***
**See Mr. McKenna's reply to Mr. Robert Harcourt, House of Commons, February 8, 1910.
***See "Times", January 3, 1910.

After the scare, the Coventry Ordnance Works secured the orders it desired, but, with singular ingratitude, it dispensed with the further services of Mr. Mulliner.

The fear inspired by the scare, and by Mr. Balfour's speeches on the Navy in the following months, did much to persuade the English people that war with Germany could not be permanently avoided. The effect on the popular imagination survived, and so did the effect in Germany produced by an official charge of underhand dealing preferred against Germany by our Government.

The view now widely prevalent in England, that Germany, for many pears past, has been deliberately, without provocation, planning and preparing for the present war, is not one which, in view of the facts, can be maintained.* It is clear that there were men in Germany, at first few, but gradually more and more, who expected war and prepared for it and even desired it. There were such men also in England, in France, and in Russia, though in the end probably not so many as in Germany. The way to diminish the number of such men would have been to show that every legitimate German aspiration would not be opposed by other Powers. Instead of adopting this method, we made it plain, by our opposition to Germany's colonial ambitions, by our policy of Ententes, and by our suspicions and reckless accusations, that Germany's aims, even when they were exactly similar to our own, could only be secured by force or

---

*This view is taken by Professor Murray in the last section but one of his pamphlet, called "The Peril in the Background."

by a terrifying threat of force. All the evidence goes
to show that in July, 1914, Germany supposed her
threat of force so terrifying that Austria would be
allowed to attack Serbia without interference. I do
not in any way palliate the crime of Germany and
Austria in so acting as to bring on war; but it is
evident that the policy of the Triple Entente, throughout the previous years, had been such as to encourage
the warlike elements in Germany, by showing on our
side a readiness for war, an amazing unscrupulousness, and a desire to thwart Germany in ways in which
no wise statesman would have wished to thwart her.
If I had been a German, I should have done all in
my power to discourage German ambitions, which I
consider foolish and brutal; being English, I should
have wished to show that England's ambitions were
of a nobler kind. But the history of the past years
shows that our ambitions were of the same kind as
those of Germany, and only our methods were different.

How are we to prevent a repetition of this long
history of deceit, cruelty, and preparation for war?
The English people is, I believe, the most humane,
generous, and peace-loving in the world:* consciously
and of set purpose, it would never tolerate such a
policy as its chosen rulers have carried on for the
last eleven years. But public attention was en-
grossed by the struggle in home politics: the fight
over the Budget, the Parliament Act, and Home Rule
made Radicals in Parliament unwilling to discredit
the Government, and unable to obtain a hearing for

*Except, perhaps, the people in America.

such criticism as they attempted. The first and most indispensable requisite, if this nation and others are not again to be led blindfolded into crime and disaster, is that everywhere men should learn to be interested in foreign affairs, to follow them closely, and to bring the pressure of public opinion to bear upon diplomacy. The war, we may hope, will have taught the democracies this lesson, that they cannot safely permit themselves to ignore dealings with foreign countries, or blindly follow the lead of men who say they deserve their trust.

The next thing to be achieved is to destroy the evil tradition of "continuity" in foreign policy. This tradition, like much that is worst in modern Liberalism, is due to Lord Roseberry. In the days of Gladstone and Disraeli, Palmerton and Lord Derby, Fox and Pitt, Chatham and Lord North, and right back to the time of the Stuarts, the parties were hotly divided on foreign policy. The absence of division dates from Gladstone's retirement, when Lord Rosebery dramatically dropped the agitation against Armenian massacres. Continuity represents no real need of national safety, but merely a closing up of the ranks among the governing classes against their common enemy the people. Ever since 1832, the upper classes of England have been faced with the problem of retaining as much as possible of the substance of power while abandoning the forms to the clamour of democrats. They have gradually lost control over legislation, while retaining in the main their hold of the administrative and judicial sides of government. In foreign affairs, their ascendancy, threatened by the Manchester school and Gladstone, was completely recovered twenty years ago, and survived, as we have seen, even the collapse of 1906. Only by reintroducing foreign affairs into the arena of party politics can this ascendancy be destroyed.

So long as both the great Parties pursue the same foreign policy, there can be no continuous effective critisism. Effective criticism, criticism which shall be heard and felt throughout the length and breadth of the land, is only possible, at normal times, when it is voiced by well-known politicians and echoed by widely-read newspapers. The criticisms of back-bench Members can always be disposed of by the simple process of not answering or reporting them. There cannot, in the long run, be any effective democratic control of foreign affairs unless prominent statesmen and newspapers are divided and are engaged in mutual criticism. But it is possible, at times when the nation is strongly stirred, for public opinion to impose a policy on a Party, as opposition to Chinese Labour was imposed on the reluctant Liberals in 1905, or as Free Trade was forced on Sir Robert Peel in 1845. This must be attempted, in regard to our diplomacy, when the present war is at an end. Perhaps it may prove a less formidable undertaking than most people would now suppose.

The interests of the British democracy do not conflict at any point with the interests of mankind. The interests of the British governing classes conflict at many points with the interests of mankind. The conquest of a new colony does not raise the wages of British labour, but it affords posts for younger sons and attractive investments for capitalists. For this reason, a policy of adventure and national prestige appeals most forcibly to the rich, while the wage-earning class, if it understood its own interests and were not caught by the glamour of Jingo phrases, would insist upon a policy of peace and international conciliation. It is to be hoped that, when the democracy realises, as it now will, its vital interest in foreign policy, it will compel the Party representing it to adopt such a programme as all friends of humanity would desire.   \

If our foreign policy is to become democratic, its aims must become such as to further the welfare of the democracy at home, and in consequence such as will not injure foreign nations.

The aims of our foreign policy must become genuinely unaggressive, and such diplomatic and financial influence as we exert on foreign countries must be in furtherance of peace and freedom.

The first step should be to announce that the British Empire is large enough, and that we firmly intend not to occupy any new parts of the earth's surface.* Alike in times of war and in times of peace, the British Empire has steadily grown and is still growing. Germany, which we regard as far more aggressive than ourselves, would be amply satisfied

---

*Professor Murray says: "The first principle of the present agreed and continuous Foreign Policy is that we seek no increase of territory." It may be that we do not seek it, but Germans may be pardoned for pointing out that we always get it. In this war, apart from annexing Cyprus and declaring a protectorate in Egypt, we have conquered German South West Africa, Togoland, German New Guinea, Samoa, and many places of less importance. If we are as successful as we hope to be, we shall keep all these (except perhaps Togoland), and probably also Mesopotamia.

if its colonial possessions increased at half the rate at which ours have increased during the last forty years. The desire for colonies is essentially a folly, based partly on vanity, partly on economic mistakes. Let us announce that we regard it in that light, and that we have no desire to increase the immense territory which we now hold. Let us announce also that we will not again, as in the case of Morocco, promise military and naval support to any other Power for purposes of colonial conquest. We should then be left with no cause for fighting except genuine self-defence.

Self-defence depends mainly upon the Navy, and no defensive policy is possible for us without a Navy strong enough to defeat any probable aggressor. But the Navy is a weapon of offence as well as of defence, and it is in its offensive capacity that it is disliked abroad. Its powers of offence are chiefly two: it enables us to conquer an enemy's colonies, and it enables us to capture his trade. If we genuinely ceased to desire new colonies, the first of these offensive powers would become unimportant. The second ought to be definitely abandoned by surrendering the right of capture at sea. Before the war, this right was upheld by the English and German Admiralties* as a means of reconciling their subject populations to the burdens of naval expenditure. For offensive purposes, as we see at the present moment,

---

*Before the war, Liberal opinion was against the maintenance of this right. On the recent attitude (before the war) of the German Admiralty, see Mr. J. H. Robertson's Introduction to Wehberg's "Right to Capture on Land and at Sea," a most useful book, by a man who is now being persecuted by the German Government on account of his fair-mindedness.

it is a powerful weapon. But for defensive purposes it is a positive weakness, since it would render fatal even the briefest loss of our command of the sea. The Germans are now clamouring for its abolition. If we abandoned it, our Navy would become obviously defensive, and would cease to be a threat to foreign commence. Probably a naval agreement with Germany could easily be embodied in the Peace in return for our abandonment of this barbarous practise.

In our relations with foreign States, we ought to endeavour to conclude arbitration treaties such as the one we have recently concluded with America. We ought to make it clear that we shall not engage in war except when we are attacked,* and we ought to avoid all such alliances and understandings as might lead foreign Powers to expect armed support from us in the event of their being at war. Such diplomatic and financial pressure as we should be able to exert without threatening war ought not to be given to certain nations regarded as "friends" and withheld from certain others regarded as at least potential "enemies." It ought to be given according to democratic principles, for the support of freedom and peace, not for the support of this or that State regardless of its behaviour. If we had followed this course in 1906, it is probable that Russia would now be a Liberal Power. If we had followed it in 1911, Persia would, in all likelihood, be free, prosperous, and Parliamentary. If we had followed

---

*Unless an International League of Great Powers could be formed to resist all aggression everywhere, and to insist upon the peaceful settlement of disputes. In that case, we might be willing to participate in a war to enforce its decisions.

it in regard to Morocco, neither the Tangier crisis nor the Agadir crisis would have occurred, and Franco-German relations would have continued, as before 1904, to become more friendly and less dominated by hopes of the *"revanche."*

A rich creditor nation, such as England, has, without the threat of war, enormous influence in international affairs through its power of granting or withholding loans. This power, hitherto, has become subordinated to the diplomatic game. But it might be used, as Palmerston used naval power, to further liberal ideas, to prevent oppression, and to promote the growth of democracy. In this way, we should not only assist to make the world at large a happier place, but we should secure the warm friendship of progressive parties and nations everywhere, as we secured the friendship of Italy and Greece by assisting them in their struggle for liberation. This role is worthy of a great and free people: to lead the nations peacefully along the road to freedom, to be not merely the most astute politicians in the tragic and futile game of armed force, but effective pioneers in the aspiration towards international peace and concord. This is the role of true glory, of true honour, and, at the same time, the surest and bravest policy for our own prosperity and safety. Generosity and wisdom alike urge this course; against it, stand the money market and aristocratic prejudice. Which will the nation follow?

## APPENDIX A.

Press Interpretations of Our Guarantee to Belgium
in 1887.

On Feb. 4, 1887, The Standard contained a letter
signed "Diplomaticus", and a leading article which
"is generally believed to have been semi-official".*
The letter was as follows:

### THE NEUTRALITY OF BELGIUM.

To the Editor of the Standard,

Sir:—It is with no wish to add to the fears that
prevail on all sides at the present moment, but simply from a desire, which I think you will hold to be
pardonable, that the English people should reflect,
in good time, what may prove to be the nature and
extent of their difficulties and responsibilities in the
event of war between France and Germany, that I
take up my pen to urge you to lay before them the
following considerations.

Military experts are of opinion that France has
spent so much money, and spent it so well, during
the last sixteen years in providing herself with a fresh
military frontier, that a direct advance by the German Armies into France, past the new fortresses
and forts that have been erected and linked together,
would be, even if a possible, a very hazardous undertaking.

But if Germany was, or considered itself to be,
provoked into a struggle of life and death with

---

*"England's Guarantee to Belgium and Luxemburg", by C. P.
Sanger and H. T. J. Norton. Allen and Unwin, 1915, page 99.

France, would Prince Bismarck, with the mighty
forces he can set in motion, consent to be baffled by
the artificial obstacles to which I have alluded, so
long as there existed a natural and undefended road
by which he could escape from his embarrassment?

Such a road or way out does exist. It lies on Belgian territory. But the neutraliy of Belgium is protected by European guarantee, and England is one of
the Guarantors.

In 1870 Earl Granville, then at the head of the
British Foreign Office, alive to this danger, promptly
and wisely bound England to side with France if
Prussia violated Belgian territory, and to side with
Prussia if France did so.

Would Lord Salisbury act prudently to take upon
himself a similar engagement, in the event of a fresh
conflict between those two countries? It is for English
men to answer the question. But it seems to me, as
one not indifferent to the interests and greatness of
England, that such a course at the present
moment would be unwise to the last degree. However
much England might regret the invasion of Belgian
territory by either party to the struggle, she could not
take part with France against Germany (even if Germany were to seek to turn the French flank by pouring
its Armies through the Belgian Ardennes), without
utterly vitiating and destroying the main purposes of
English policy all over the world.

But, it will be asked, must not England honour its
signature and be faithful to its public pledges? I
reply that your Foreign Minister ought to be equal to
the task of meeting this objection without committing

England to war. The temporary use of a right of way is something different from a permanent and wrongful possession of territory; and surely England would easily be able to obtain from Prince Bismarck ample and adequate guarantees that at the close of the conflict, the territory of Belgium should remain intact as before?

You will see, Sir, that I raise, in a very few words, an exceedingly important question. It is for the English people to perpend and pronounce. But it is high time they reflected on it.

I am, Sir,

Your obedient servant,

Diplomaticus.

Feb. 2.

The article in the "Standard" ran as follows:

"We are reminded this morning, by a Correspondent who speaks with high authority, that while we are all wondering how long it will be before a fresh conflict breaks out between France and Germany, Englishmen are shutting their eyes to a question closely, and perhaps inevitably, allied with that contingent event, and affecting the interests of this country more vitally than they could be affected even by any probable result from the struggle between those two powerful States. "Diplomaticus" writes with unprofessional terseness; but his observations are to the point, and are expressed with significant lucidity. Nor can there be any doubt as to the nature or as to the gravity of the question raised in his communication. In the event of war between Germany and France, and in case either Germany or France were to disregard the neutrality of Belgian territory, what ought England to do? That is the question, and he indicates pretty plainly a reply with which, we may say at once, we do not believe the English people will be disposed to quarrel. In order, however, to enable them to respond to the inquiry with full knowledge and deliberate judgment, it is necessary to lay before them the facts and contingencies of the situation somewhat more amply and more *in extenso* than is done by "Diplomaticus." On the Declaration of War by France against Prussia, in 1870, Earl Granville, as we all know, with more promptness and decision than he usually displayed, sought to secure respect for Belgian territory by notifying that, should either combatant ignore the neutrality secured to it by public treaty, England would side actively with the other combatant. It may be said, why cannot the same course be pursued once more, in the event of a similar condition of affairs coming into play? The answer is that a similar condition of affairs no longer exists. In the first place, in 1870 neither of the combatants had any pressing temptation to resort to a violation of Belgian territory, in the execution of their military designs. The territory of Germany was avowedly vulnerable in several places; and France was so assured of its military superiority, and so confident that "A Berlin!" not "Nach Paris!" would prove the successful war cry of the struggle, that no precautions had been taken against the possibility of France being invaded. As the event proved, even such magnificent fortresses as Metz and Strasburg, with their large civil population and their imperfect stores of provisions, proved an encumbrance and a source of danger rather than one of safety; and, these once invested, there was nothing to stop the march of the victors of Sedan towards the French capital. Metz and Strasburg are now German fortresses; and no one requires to be told that Germany has neglected no precautions or expedients to render an invasion of the territory of the Fatherland a difficult if not an impracticable undertaking. Armed to the head for offence, Germany is likewise armed to the heel for defence. She is more invulnerable than Achilles, for there is no point uncovered.

How stands it with France as regards defence against invasion? During the last sixteen years all that money profusely spent, and military skill judiciously applied, could do to provide her with a strong military frontier against Germany, has been quietly, but steadily and unremittingly, carried forward. Not only does France possess a first line of fortresses, contiguous to German territory, in Belfort, Epinal, Toul, and Verdun; but all four are linked with each other, in succession, by another line of detached forts. Not to encumber ourselves here with military details, the full exposition of which would demand considerable space, we may say that "Diplomaticus" is guilty of no exaggeration when he declares that military experts are of opinion that France has spent so much money, and spent it so well, since the last war in providing herself with a fresh military frontier, that a direct advance by the German Armies into France past the new fortresses and forts that have been erected and linked together would be, even if a possible, a very hazardous undertaking. There are, however, two other ways of entering France from Germany. One is through Switzerland; the other is through Belgium. Both are what is understood by "neutral territory"; but the mountainous character of Switzerland renders access to France through its passes more arduous and less available than through the territory of Belgium. In case the German armies found themselves practically prevented from engaging in offensive military operations against France by the admirable line of defence with which she has provided herself, would Prince Bismarck, and the great soldiers whom he would inspire, consent to be thwarted by the inviolability of Belgium as guaranteed by European Treaty? "Diplomaticus" puts the question with undiplomatic bluntness. He forbears from answering it; and so must we. But it will be obvious to everybody that there is a possibility, a danger, of Germany not being willing to be debarred from invading France by an obstacle that has grown up since the Treaty guaranteeing the neutrality of Belgium was signed. Our readers will at once perceive that the situation is absolutely different from the one that existed in 1870, when Earl Granville quickly and cheerfully imposed on England the obligation to take part against either combatants that violated Belgian soil. Neither combatant was much tempted to do so; and thus the engagement assumed by England—a very proper one at the time—was not very serious or onerous, and saved appearances rather than created responsibility. Now the position is entirely changed. If England, with a view to securing respect for Belgian territory, were to bind itself, as in 1870, to throw its weight into the balance against either France or Germany, should either France or Germany violate Belgian ground, we might, and probably should, find ourselves involved in a war of giants on our own account.

We think that "Diplomaticus" understands the English people when he hints his suspicions that such a result would be utterly alien alike to their wishes and to their interests. For, over and above the fact that, as we have seen, the temptation to violate Belgian territory by either side is much greater than it was in 1870, the relations of England with the European Powers have necessarily and naturally undergone considerable modification during that period. We concur with our correspondent in the opinion he expresses that for England and Germany to quarrel, it matters not upon what subject, would be highly injurious to the interests of both. Indeed, he is right when he says that the main outlines of our policy would be blurred and its main purposes embarrassed, if not defeated, were we suddenly to find ourselves in a state of hostility to Germany, instead of one of friendliness and sympathy. No doubt, if Germany were to outrage the honour, or to disregard the interests, of England, we should be ready enough to accept the challenge thrown down to us. But would the violation of Belgian territory, whether by Germany or France, be such an injury to our interests? It might be so, in certain circumstances; and it would assuredly be so if it involved a permanent violation of the independence of Belgium. But, as "Diplomaticus" ingeniously suggests, there is all the difference in the world between the momentary use of a 'right of way,' even if the use of the right of way be, in a sense, wrongful, and the appropriation of the ground covered by the right of way. We trust that both Germany and France would refrain even from this minor trespass. But if they did not? If one or the other were to say to England, 'All the military approaches to France and Germany have been closed; and only neutral approaches lie open to us. This state of things is not only detrimental, but fatal to our military success, and it has arisen since the Treaty guaranteed the sacredness of the only road of which we can now avail ourselves. We will, as a fact, respect the independence of Belgium and we will give you the most solemn and binding guarantees that, at the end of the conflict, Belgium shall be as free and independent as before.' If Germany,—and, of course, our hypothesis applies also to France—were to use this language— though we trust there will be no occasion for it—we cannot doubt what would be the wise and proper course for England to pursue, and what would be the answer of the English Government. England does not wish to shirk its true responsibilities. But it would be madness for us to incur or assume responsibilities unnecessarily, when to do so would manifestly involve our participation in a tremendous War.''

On the same day the ''Pall Mall Gazette,'' then Liberal, published the following article:

### ENGLAND AND BELGIUM.
#### Are We Bound to Intervene?
#### There Is No Guarantee.

''The 'Standard' this morning gives special prominence to a letter signed 'Diplomaticus,' on the neutrality of Belgium. It also devotes its first leading article to the subject. The gist of these utterances may be summed up in two propositions: (1) England is under a treaty of obligation to defend the neutrality of Belgium; (2) But circumstances have altered since the contraction of the said obligation, and as against Germany, at any rate, England must pocket its pledges, and allow France to be invaded through Belgium without protesting or interfering.

''Considerable importance is likely to be attached to these conclusions abroad owing to its being understood that the 'Standard' is at present the Governmental and Salisburian organ. Each of the propositions laid down by our contemporary is, it will be seen, likely to be taken hold of. Germany might read the second as an invitation to invade France through Belgium; France might read the first as an admission of our obligation to prevent, or rather to punish, such an infringement of neutral territory, *if we dared*.

''It becomes important, therefore, to point out that the 'Standard's' argument rests on a false asumption. We do not for the present argue whether in the contingencies contemplated it would be England's *interest* to intervene by declaring war against whichever belligerent might violate the neutrality of Belgium; we confine ourselves to the preliminary statement—essential for clearing up the case—that it is not England's *obligation* to do so.

''The origin of the mistaken views prevailing on the question is undoubtedly a confusion between the Special Treaty of 1870 and the preceding General Treaties of 1831 and 1839 which it temporarily superceded. By the treaty of 1870 the obligation of England was, of course, clear and specific. Here is the pledge which was given in the identical treaties concluded *mutatis mutandis* with both France and Prussia:

" 'Her Majesty the Queen of the United Kingdom of Great Britain and Ireland declares that if during the said hostilities the armies of France (or Prussia) should violate the neutrality of Belgium, she will be prepared to co-operate with his Prussian Majesty (or the Emperor of the French) for the defence of the same in such manner as may be mutually agreed upon, employing for that purpose her naval and military forces to ensure its observance.'

"There could be no doubt about that pledge; but then it expired twelve months after the conclusion of peace. At the expiration of that period, so the treaty continued:

" 'The independence and neutrality of Belgium will, so far as the High Contracting Parties are respectively concerned, continue to rest as heretofore on the first article of the Quintuple Treaty of the 19th of April, 1839.'

"Now, what some people do is to read this treaty of 1839 by the light of the more specific treaty of 1870, and to deduce from the former the same obligation on the part of England to intervene against any infringement of Belgium's neutrality as was contained in the 1870 treaty.

"This, however, is a completely untenable proceeding. The treaty of 1839 must stand on its own legs, and these, it will be seen, are by no means very strong. The following are the terms of its second article:

" 'H. M. the Emperor of Austria, King of Hungary and Bohemia, H. M. the King of the French, H. M. the Queen of the United Kingdom of Great Britain and Ireland, H. M. the King of Prussia, and H. M. the Emperor of ALL the Russias, declare that the articles hereby annexed to the treaty concluded this day between his Majesty the King of the Belgians and his Majesty the King of the Netherlands, Grand Duke of Luxemberg, are considered as having the same force and value as if they were textually inserted in the present Act, and that they were thus placed under the guarantee of their Majesties.'

"Here, then, we are sent off from the treaty between the Great Powers to the treaty between Belgium and the Netherlands. The seventh article of this treaty (which is identical with the same article of the 1831 treaty) runs:

" 'Belgium will form, within the limits indicated in 1, 2, and 4, an independent and perpetually neutral State. She will be bound to observe this same neutrality towards all other States.'

"In this treaty it will be seen there is nothing about any guarantee; all that can be elicited from it, and from the one cited as referring to it, is this, that this clause is placed under the guarantee of 'their said Majesties,' that is, England, Austria, France, Germany, and Russia.

"But that is not all. This constructive guarantee must be considered in relation to the party to whom it was given—namely, to the Netherlands. For the treaty of 1839 was one between the five Powers on the one hand and the Netherlands on the other; and what the five Powers did was to guarantee to the Netherlands the treaty contracted between it and Belgium, one clause of which treaty said that Belgium should form 'an independent and perpetually neutral State,' and should 'be bound to observe such neutrality towards all other States.'

"In the treaty of 1831, it is true, there was a further article guaranteeing the execution of all preceding articles (including, therefore, the one just cited in similar terms from the 1839 treaty) to the King of the Belgians, but in the 1839 treaty, on which the independence of Belgium is now said to rest, Lord Palmerston omitted any such guarantee.

*"There is, therefore, no English guarantee to Belgium. It is possible, perhaps, to 'construct' such a guarantee; but the case may be summed up as follows:* (1) *England is under no guarantee whatever except such as is common to Austria, France, Russia, and Germany;* (2) *that guarantee is not specifically of the neutrality of Belgium at all; and* (3) *is given not to Belgium but to the Netherlands."*

The "Spectator," on Feb. 5, said:

". . . the general idea (is) that England will keep out of this (war). . . That she will try to do so we do not doubt, but there is the Belgian difficulty ahead. Our guarantee for her is not a solitary one, and would not bind us to fight alone; but there are general interests to be considered. The probability is that we shall insist on her not becoming a theatre

of war but shall not bar—as indeed we cannot bar—
the traversing of her soil."

The above extracts are reprinted in Sanger **and**
Norton, (*op. cit.*) and in the "Labour Leader" of
Feb. 4, 1915. Messrs. Sanger & Norton sum up their
discussion as follows:

"From all the evidence it is clear that in the past
the British Government has not considered that the
Treaty of 1839 imposed a binding obligation to go to
war with any Power which infringed the neutrality of
Belgium" (p. 109).

## APPENDIX B.

What Support Did We Offer to France in 1905?

The evidence as to our attitude during 1905 consists partly of leading articles in "The Times", partly of revelations in the "Figaro" and the "Matin" in October, 1905, partly of Sir Edward Grey's confession that he authorised military and naval conversations with the French in January, 1906, during the General Election of that month.

"The Times" is universally believed on the Continent to be inspired by the Foreign Office, and careful readers will find that, until the last few months, it has invariably, in its articles on foreign affairs, represented the policy of the Foreign Office whenever it is known what that policy was. It is natural to suppose that it has also represented the Foreign office at times when the policy of the Foreign Office is not otherwise known. Now from the moment of the Kaiser's first demand for a Conference, "The Times" opposed the very idea. Never once did it hint that Germany was "justified in asking for a Conference", as Professor Murray now concedes. Everything that "The Times" could do, it did, to encourage France to resist the German demands, and to make France feel that our support would be given whatever the consequences of resistance might be.*

Sir Edward Grey, in his speech on August 3, 1914, told us that, in January, 1906, just when the Algeciras

*See "Times", April 6, June 16, 1905.

Conference was assembling, a sudden crisis arose, and he, at the request of the French, authorised the discussion of plans for military and naval co-operation in the event of England and France being jointly involved in war with Germany. He gave this authorisation after consulting only three other members of the Cabinet; the Cabinet as a whole, by his own confession, was not informed of his action until a much later time. Now the occurrence of these conversations at this time proves that we were at any rate not opposed in principle to the military support of France in its policy of Moroccan conquest, even if that policy should entail all the horrors from which Europe is now suffering.

The remaining evidence is contained in revelations made by the *"Matin"* and the *"Figaro,"* of which the substance may be read in *"The Times"* of October, 1905. *"The Times"* of Oct. 9, 1905, contains the following note from its Paris Correspondent on the *Matin* revelations concerning the proceedings at the Council of Ministers which ended in M. Delcassé's resignation.

"He (M. Delcassé) declared that France could not go to the proposed international conference (i. e. Algeciras that was to be) without belittling herself and running the risk of submitting to the discussion of Third Powers two agreements which bore her signature and which had been ratified by her Parliament. He furnished documentary evidence that England, Spain, Italy, Russian and the United States were ready to refuse their adhesion to the Conference scheme. . . . He further informed his colleagues that Great Britain was ready, whatever might happen, to back up France to the very end, and that in the improbable eventuality of an unexpected aggression Great Britain would side with her. In a footnote the Editor of the *Matin* states that England verbally informed the French government that, if France was attacked, she was ready to mobilise her fleet, to seize the Kiel canal, and to land 100,000 men in Schleswig-Holstein, and that the French Government was subsequently informed that if they wished it this offer would be made in writing."

"*The Times*" leading article on this says:

"M. Delcassé, it (the "Matin") affirms, informed his colleagues that England was ready to support France and that in the event of an unexpected act of aggression directed against France, England would side with the Republic. With that statement we have no fault to find. We do not all doubt that in such a contingency the English Government would have supported France with the hearty approval of the nation. But we very much doubt the further announcement which the *Matin* makes upon its own responsibility that England had verbally informed the French Government that she was prepared to take certain specific action in that contingency. We believe on the contrary that the French Government very wisely refrained from asking for any assurances of the kind mentioned."

On *Oct. 13th,* the Paris Correspondent notes that Jaurès declared in a speech at Limoges that he knew things did really take place as stated.

On *Oct. 13th,* the Paris Correspondent says that

Jaurès has written in *l'Humanité*: I was not aware that it was in Schleswig-Holstein that England was to land 100,000 men, but, with the exception of this precise statement, I heard at the moment of the crisis from a direct and safe French source everything that M. Delcassé said at the Council of Ministers as to the intervention offered by England. I heard at the time that she wanted to engage herself towards us, even by a written treaty, to support us against Germany, not only by the mobilisation of the Fleet, but by the landing of 100,000 men."

On *Oct. 14th*, the Paris Correspondent writes that the following semi-official note is published by the Havas Agency:

"We are authorised to declare that the accounts which have appeared in the newspapers as to the incidents that accompanied the retirement of M. Delcassé and particularly the details as to the Ministerial Council which preceded this retirement are inaccurate."

The correspondent goes on to say: "The Editor of the *'Matin'*, M. Stephane Lauzanne, declares that every line which appeared over his signature and which described what took place at the Council of Ministers on June 6 was strictly accurate. M. Lauzanne refers to the speech delivered by M. Jaurès at Limoges on Sunday and to the article published on Thursday in *l'Humanité*. . . . He also invokes the testimony of the *"Daily Mail"* of yesterday and of the *"Petite Republique"* of the same date. . . . 'For three days past', says M. Louzanne— 'Prince Bülow's press has been calling upon the Eng-

lish and French Governments to contradict officially.
. . . To this summons the British government
replies by a contemptuous shrug of the shoulders
but the French Government bows before the order
coming from the other side of the Rhine. The note
communicated to-day has a new name. It is not
called a *démenti*. It is called *'une complaisance.'* "
The Paris Correspondent continues to note that the
*"Figaro"* gives facts of the British offer during the
year which elapsed after the conclusion of the Anglo-
French Agreement. "The British Government," it
says, "approached our diplomatists on three occasions in order to ascertain whether France was willing to conclude a definite treaty of alliance. The
French Government, from regard no doubt for Russia, who was engaged in a war with Great Britain's
ally, declined to take this question into consideration.
But when the Franco-German conflict reached an
acute stage, French diplomacy took up the question
for itself. Our Ambassador in London, M. Cambon,
obtained from Lord Lansdowne the verbal assurance
of effective support from England in the event of a
conflagration, and M. Cambon was able to announce
to M. Delcassé that, the *casus foederis* once given,
Great Britain would reiterate this assurance in writing. Thus it was that about the 15th of June, Lord
Lansdowne was able to declare to some friends that
in the event of a Franco-German war, there would
not be the least doubt about the intervention of Great
Britain. I was told in Berlin from a highly official
source that Germany had been informed of these
events towards the middle of May by Count Wolff-

Metternich, the German Ambassador in London." The German Emperor, the *Figaro* writer goes on to say, took immediate action by communicating the information through Italy to France, thus bringing about the resignation of M. Delcassé.

The same note goes on to state that:

"Reuter's Agency is enabled to state authoritatively with regard to the recent sensational revelations in the French Press that Germany has been informed by Great Britain that the question of the latter's offering assistance to France never arose, that France never asked for assistance and further that Great Britain never offered it."

"On enquiry in British Government circles with reference to the above, Reuter's Agency is informed that His Majesty's Government is not making any statement on the subject."

The *"Times"* leading article on the 16th of Oct. says:

"We do not know, and we do not pretend to know, how the French nation came to understand, as they did understand with good reason, that in the event of an unprovoked attack upon them arising out of the Anglo-French Agreement we should support them. But as M. Clemenceau argues with unanswerable force in the *Aurore,* what conceivable grounds can Germany or any other peaceable power have to complain of that?

"Our support would be given only in the case of unprovoked aggression. Germany declares that she never dreams of unprovoked aggression against anybody and certainly not against France at the present time. Why then does she cry out?

"That the French ever asked for assurances of our intervention, or that we ever gratuitously offered them, we do not for a moment believe. That the Germans should be exceedingly inquisitive as to our relations with France is not surprising. That they will discover anything more than has already been openly proclaimed to the world we do not think likely."

On *Oct. 27*, the Paris correspondent says that:

"M. Andre Mévil in *Echo de Paris* writes: 'Towards the middle of June we informed England that the ill-will of Germany became daily more evident and that the crisis, instead of passing away, was only being aggravated. On June 20, M. Paul Cambon, who had spent 48 hours in Paris, returned to London, with precise instructions from the French Government. On the afternoon of the 21st he had a long conversation with Lord Lansdowne at the Foreign Office, in the course of which he informed him of the situation. When once the British government knew exactly what was taking place they decided to intervene energetically. I remember that on the evening of June 21 a rumour was current in London that next day, or the day after at the latest, Count Wolff-Metternich, the German Ambassador in London, would have a significant interview with Lord Lansdowne. Being in London at the time I heard the news. The truth is that Lord Lansdowne had officially declared to Count Wolff-Metternich that if ever Germany attacked France, all the military forces of the British Empire would come to the assistance of the latter. Thus twice in less than a month England had offered her support to France.' ''

None of this evidence is conclusive on either side, and I have not found any way of arriving at certainty as to our promises in 1905.

# INDEX